DIVORCE
SOS

ECHO SKY
PUBLISHING

ECHO SKY PUBLISHING
Boca Raton, FL 33498

ISBNs:

eBook	979-8-9994956-2-4
Paperback	979-8-9994956-1-7
Hardcover	979-8-9994956-0-0
Library of Congress Control Number:	2025915968

First Edition
Book Production and Publishing by Brands Through Books
brandsthroughbooks.com

Echoskypublishing.com

AMY SHIELD, ESQ., and ROGER LEVINE, ESQ.

Highest-Rated Attorneys

DIVORCE
SOS

HOW TO **AVOID** COSTLY MISTAKES AND **PROTECT** YOUR MONEY, CHILDREN, AND SANITY

ECHO SKY PUBLISHING

PRAISE FOR *DIVORCE SOS*

"This book offers a detailed guide to the divorce process for people who are either contemplating or in the midst of divorce proceedings. It empowers readers with practical advice and essential information throughout the process, including critical dos and don'ts at each stage. While it doesn't replace personalized legal counsel, it ensures that individuals will have a comprehensive understanding of the complexities of the divorce process and will be well equipped to avoid common mistakes that could have long-term consequences. With my 50 years as a trial lawyer and a circuit judge, this is a must-read for anyone getting a divorce."

—DAVID E. FRENCH, Mediator and Retired Judge, 15th Judicial Circuit of Florida

"I've known Amy Shield for years professionally as one of Florida's top family law appellate attorneys, and I can't recommend *Divorce SOS* highly enough. Cowritten with her son, Roger Levine—another outstanding attorney—this book reflects the deep legal wisdom that quite literally runs in the family. With clarity, compassion, and an easy-to-read style, *Divorce SOS* is a must-read for anyone navigating the often overwhelming process of divorce. Drawing from their extensive legal experience, Amy and Roger translate critical legal and practical advice into real world guidance. They cover how to avoid costly mistakes, protect your finances and your children, and set yourself up for the best possible outcome. Their collaborative voice adds a personal, reassuring touch that leaves readers feeling informed, empowered, and genuinely supported through every step of the journey."

—VICKY TOWNSEND, President and Founder of Divorce Right, Inc. and Bridgewell EAP

"As President and Founder of the National Association of Divorce Professionals, I value resources that offer both practical advice and meaningful insight. Divorce SOS stands out for its clear guidance, relatable examples, and the depth of legal experience behind it. Amy Shield and Roger Levine's thoughtful and expertly structured approach shines through every chapter, making even the most complex topics easy to understand and apply. Whether you are going through a divorce yourself or supporting clients who are, this book is absolutely worth reading."

—LIZ BECKER, President & Founder, National Association of Divorce Professionals (NADP) and The Certified Divorce Specialist (CDS®) Program

To Frank Fishman and in memory of Helen Shield Fox,
for all their love and unwavering support.

TABLE OF CONTENTS

INTRODUCTION   1

PART 1.   MISTAKES TO AVOID BEFORE YOU FILE   7
            FOR DIVORCE

CHAPTER 1. CHANGE YOUR PASSWORDS!   9

CHAPTER 2. COMMON MISTAKES MADE IN EMAILING,   15
            TEXTING, AND SOCIAL MEDIA

CHAPTER 3. PROTECT YOUR PHYSICAL WELL-BEING   25
            AND SANITY

CHAPTER 4. HOW TO PICK YOUR DIVORCE LAWYER   31

CHAPTER 5. THE IMPORTANCE OF BEING UP-FRONT   39
            AND HONEST WITH YOUR LAWYER

CHAPTER 6. MEDIATION; ARBITRATION;   43
            COLLABORATIVE, UNCONTESTED, AND
            CONTESTED DIVORCES—HOW ARE THEY
            DIFFERENT?

PART 2.   MISTAKES TO AVOID DURING YOUR   49
            DIVORCE PROCEEDINGS

CHAPTER 7. DOES IT REALLY MATTER WHO FILES   51
            FIRST?

CHAPTER 8. DRESS AND DECORUM IN THE   55
            COURTROOM AND ONLINE HEARINGS

CHAPTER 9. THE DOS AND DON'TS FOR SUCCESSFUL   59
            DEPOSITIONS AND HEARINGS

CHAPTER 10. IF A COURT REPORTER DIDN'T TRANSCRIBE IT, IT DIDN'T HAPPEN!   71

CHAPTER 11. THE DOS AND DON'TS OF PARENTING DURING DIVORCE PROCEEDINGS   75

CHAPTER 12. PARENTING PLANS—COMMONLY OVERLOOKED PROVISIONS   89

CHAPTER 13. CHILDREN'S THERAPISTS, ATTORNEYS AD LITEM, GUARDIANS AD LITEM, AND SOCIAL INVESTIGATIONS   105

CHAPTER 14. THE IMPORTANCE OF KNOWING YOUR FINANCES   113

CHAPTER 15. COMMON MISTAKES MADE IN PREPARING FINANCIAL AFFIDAVITS   121

CHAPTER 16. THE MARITAL RESIDENCE—STAY, LEAVE, OR SELL?   139

CHAPTER 17. BUSINESS INTERESTS—HOW THEY ARE VALUED   151

CHAPTER 18. WHO GETS THE FAMILY PET?   159

CHAPTER 19. DIVISION OF OTHER PROPERTIES AND OF MARITAL LIABILITIES   167

CHAPTER 20. TAX RAMIFICATIONS YOU MAY NOT HAVE THOUGHT OF   193

CHAPTER 21. ALIMONY AND CHILD SUPPORT   205

CHAPTER 22. COSTLY MISTAKES MADE IN MARITAL SETTLEMENT AGREEMENTS   217

CHAPTER 23. PRENUPTIAL AGREEMENTS AND POSTNUPTIAL AGREEMENTS   229

PART 3.	MISTAKES TO AVOID WITH APPEALS	241
CHAPTER 24.	WHAT ARE APPEALS AND WHY DO THEY MATTER?	243
CHAPTER 25.	THE NEXT STEPS NOW THAT YOU'VE BEEN THROUGH THIS JOURNEY	261
ACKNOWLEDGEMENTS		265
ABOUT THE AUTHORS		267
ENDNOTES		271

A NOTE TO THE READER

This book does not constitute legal advice, nor does it provide accounting, financial, or counseling services. The book is for general informational purposes only. There is no attorney-client relationship established between the reader and Shield & Levine, P.A. or the Firm's attorneys, who are appellate lawyers licensed to practice in Florida.

The various topics covered in this book should not be considered a complete explanation of the law. While the book strives to be accurate, there is no warranty, express or implied, and no representation as to its accuracy. The law as applied to the reader's issues may differ or change depending upon the individual's facts and jurisdiction.

This book is not a substitute for seeking qualified professional counsel for your issues. You should not act upon any of the information in this book without first consulting qualified professionals on your specific situation.

The terms *lawyer* and *attorney* are used interchangeably, and there is no significance in using one term or the other. Names and some facts have been changed to protect confidentiality. Other anecdotes are from published cases referenced in this book's endnotes. Most are based on Florida law, which is subject to change and can be slightly to significantly different from the law of other jurisdictions.

INTRODUCTION

WHY WE WROTE THIS BOOK

WE ARE MOTHER AND SON, AMY SHIELD AND ROGER LEVINE, ATTORNEYS and law partners in our firm, Shield & Levine, P.A. More than half our practice is devoted to family law appeals and assisting divorce attorneys through the litigation process. Through the years, we have seen many preventable mistakes made by spouses going through a divorce that have never been discussed in books dealing with this subject. These mistakes have resulted in devastating financial outcomes that could have been avoided, as well as heartbreaking consequences from not properly handling situations involving the parties' children.

Other than the death of a loved one, divorce is generally considered the most stressful event in a person's life. Through the many years of handling divorce appeals, we have seen the different ways people experience divorce. You may not want to face the fact that your spouse wants a divorce and might be in denial. You may be feeling depressed and overly emotional at the thought your marriage is ending and how it is going to affect you and your children. Or you may be excited about the possibilities the end of your marriage will afford you. You may be anxious and confused; fearful, angry, or frustrated; or wanting revenge. What impacts the problem is not knowing what to expect, what your best options are, and the best way to achieve your goals. We believe knowledge of what to expect and the mistakes to avoid can substantially reduce or counter some of the emotional and financial turmoil and help you to feel empowered. We also believe our background and experience make us uniquely qualified to write this book.

WE BOTH HAVE FIRSTHAND EXPERIENCE WITH DIVORCE

Amy: I have been married three times! After almost seventeen years of marriage to an attorney, my first divorce settled quickly, and we were divorced in a little more than a month after filing. I raised my son, Roger, as a single mother with primary custody. My second divorce, after a short-term marriage, resulted in a nasty court fight. Three was the charm for me, as my third marriage is a happy one, and at the time of publication, we've been together for twenty-four years.

Roger: I am a child of divorce, as my parents divorced when I was just ten years old. As a result, I can understand divorce from a child's perspective.

HOW WE BECAME SPECIALISTS IN DIVORCE LITIGATION

Amy: As a young attorney, I began practicing at a Miami law firm as their appellate attorney specializing in appeals from personal injury and medical malpractice cases. While at that firm, I argued my first case before the Supreme Court of Florida at twenty-eight years old.

After moving to Palm Beach County in 1981, with my lawyer husband and son, Roger, a contact introduced me to an attorney with a large family law practice who was interested in having me handle a divorce appeal for one of his clients. Wanting to be fully prepared, I read an entire Florida legal encyclopedia covering family law and many published cases on divorce so I would have a working knowledge of that area of the law when representing that client. I won the appeal, and thereafter, his firm referred all their family law appeals to me.

My husband and I became partners in our law firm, and for about eight years I represented both husbands and wives in their divorces in the trial court as well as on appeal, in addition to handling contract disputes and other commercial litigation in both the trial and appellate courts. Our law partnership ended with the end of our marriage, and thereafter, with the exception of a year at another law firm, I was a sole practitioner until my partnership with Roger, where the majority of our practice concerns divorce appeals.

Roger: It was natural for me to become a lawyer, when both my parents were lawyers. I clerked for a law firm that specialized in representing plaintiffs in personal injury cases, as well as a firm that handled commercial litigation, to get experience in various areas of the law. After being sworn in as an attorney, I began working at my mother's law firm, where I eventually became a full partner, working on many divorce appeals and advising divorce attorneys with their trial court cases.

OUR LEGAL EXPERIENCE

Amy: I have a vast amount of experience, having been a lawyer for 49 years. During my many years of practice, I have reviewed thousands of transcripts and countless divorce court files. I've seen costly mistakes that could easily have been avoided; that's why this book was written.

Martindale-Hubbell, considered the gold standard in attorney peer review ratings, has given me an AV Preeminent® rating for the highest level of professional excellence in legal knowledge, communication skills, and ethical standards, which is attained by only about 10 percent of attorneys in the United States[1].

As an appellate attorney, I've handled all types of civil appeals in the appellate courts throughout the State of Florida and before the Supreme Court of Florida. For family law appeals, I've represented spouses whose issues concerned alimony, child support, custody (time-sharing), division of property (equitable distribution), prenuptial and postnuptial agreements, relocation, supportive relationships, and contempt orders. Trial court judges have appointed me as a Guardian ad Litem and as an Attorney ad Litem for children in high conflict cases[2].

I am considered the lawyer's lawyer—divorce lawyers hire me and my partner, Roger Levine, to advise on difficult legal issues, provide them with the law, help prepare them for important hearings, as well as review and sometimes draft their court filings and proposed orders.

Roger: I also have an AV Preeminent® rating from Martindale-Hubbell for achieving the highest level of professional excellence in legal knowledge, communication skills, and ethical standards. Similar to my partner, Amy Shield, divorce attorneys rely on my expertise to tell them the law, answer legal questions that arise in their practice, advise them how to best protect their record and what they need to do at a hearing to give them the best chance of winning, draft memorandums of law they will give to the judges, and review legal documents and proposed orders before they are provided to the judges. When requested, I attend hearings with trial counsel to advise on the spot about intricate areas of law and make sure all important points are covered at the hearing.

I represent clients for their appeals throughout the State of Florida. While my experience is in Florida, I can provide general advice and best practices for anyone going through a divorce.

I've had a significant amount of experience in helping others in the community. After graduating law school, for about five years, I taught English and Civics to help empower low-income people through education. For approximately ten years, I served as a Guardian ad Litem to dependent children in Palm Beach County.

I have reviewed hundreds of transcripts and divorce files, and have seen many types of mistakes that could have been avoided, saving the client from additional litigation, additional expense, and additional emotional upset.

WHO SHOULD READ THIS BOOK

This book is a must-read for the person contemplating divorce who wants to have a better and clearer game plan. This book is also for the person already going through a divorce who wants to have a more successful outcome.

WHY THIS BOOK IS UNIQUE

Take a minute to look at the Table of Contents. This book provides valuable information with practical advice on various topics, dealing with all aspects of divorce, such as alimony, child support, dividing your finances, and the family home and business. It also includes many topics that are not found in other divorce books, like how to handle social media during the divorce, how best to answer questions at your deposition or while being cross-examined at trial, costly mistakes made in marital settlement agreements, who gets the family pet, and why it really does matter who files for divorce first.

OUR PROMISE TO THE READER

In our practice, we work together on all of our cases and projects. This book is no exception. We have both contributed to the many topics covered in this book that confront spouses preparing for divorce, going through a divorce, and in post-divorce litigation.

We believe knowledge is a powerful tool. Although we practice in Florida, once you read this book, you will have the knowledge to avoid many of the pitfalls and costly mistakes that commonly occur during the divorce process no matter where you live.

This book will help enable you to plan for and have a successful divorce.

PART 1

MISTAKES TO AVOID BEFORE YOU FILE FOR DIVORCE

CHANGE YOUR PASSWORDS!

MICHAEL AND PHYLLIS LED SEPARATE LIVES AS THE SPARK IN THEIR thirty-five-year marriage was long gone. Phyllis was never interested in Michael's company, and she knew very little about their financial circumstances. Phyllis had been a homemaker, primarily raising the children, and after they became empty nesters, she busied herself with gardening and going out to lunch with her lady friends. At one of the corporate conferences in his industry, Michael met Karen, and soon they were exchanging phone calls and planning get-togethers when he had to go out of town for business. Eventually, Michael decided to end his marriage, as he was now involved in a serious relationship with Karen. However, Michael did not want to share the substantial assets he had obtained during his marriage to Phyllis, so he and Karen set about a plan to hide assets and alter his income, in order to leave a smaller division of the marital assets and a lower alimony award. When not together, they corresponded by email. Phyllis did not know about Karen, and although no longer in love with Michael, she was surprised when he filed for divorce.

But Michael's planning forgot a critical detail. He never changed the password to his personal email account or the accounts he shared with his wife, who had all these passwords. After being served with the divorce papers, Phyllis began looking at Michael's online accounts and discovered Michael's relationship with Karen, along with their scheme to conceal assets and income from her. Phyllis gave copies of all the incriminating emails to her lawyer.

At trial, Michael's relationship with Karen was brought to the judge's attention, as well as the emails. To Phyllis's surprise, the judge was not concerned about the affair itself, but what really angered the judge was Michael's intent to deceive the court by not listing his accurate income or assets on the financial affidavit he filed in the divorce. This resulted in the judge readily awarding Phyllis the substantial alimony she had been seeking as well as half of all their actual marital assets.

From Michael's viewpoint, this story illustrates the importance of changing your passwords. Michael got caught trying to deceive the court and suffered the consequences by failing to change his passwords. The two morals of this story are to make sure the person you are divorcing cannot easily see what you have done online and to be honest with the court. Being exposed when not doing both of these things will make your divorce far more costly than it would have been.

DON'T FORGET TO CHANGE THE PASSWORDS TO THESE ACCOUNTS

Costly common mistakes can easily be avoided by changing all passwords to emails and social media, and especially to your phone, even if you think your spouse doesn't know these passwords. Better to be safe than sorry! You should also open a new email account for all correspondence with your divorce lawyer.

Make a list of *shared* online accounts, devices, and passwords. This includes online shopping sites, streaming services, video conferencing platforms like Zoom, airline portals, ride-sharing accounts like Lyft and Uber, hotel booking apps, and cloud storage. You may not want your spouse to know all your activities, which can easily be detected should he or she share your password. You want to have a stronger, more secure password instead of a birthday, a pet's name, or partial home address. You may also want to opt for adding a two-factor authentication process to make it more difficult for your spouse to get into your accounts. Don't use the same password for multiple sites.

Credit Cards

They may be in your name alone, but your spouse may have access to the card and password. The same goes for Venmo, PayPal, Zelle, and other e-payment services.

Discuss with your attorney whether you should close your credit card account and open a new account so your spouse has no access. In one case, there were only two weeks left before John's credit card expired in an account which his recently separated wife, Susan, had access to, so John thought it was unnecessary to close the account. Unfortunately, to John's dismay, during those two weeks Susan maxed out the $40,000 monthly credit card limit.

However, closing a credit card account may not always be the best strategy and action to take. Some spouses who would have acted responsibly with credit card access will become incensed if the accounts are closed, thereafter changing their approach to litigation from cooperation to all-out war. You need to take your knowledge of your history with your spouse and apply your actions to the facts of your case.

Credit Report

Get a copy of your credit report to find out if your spouse has opened credit cards or other accounts in your name. Joint accounts can impact your credit scores, especially if your spouse misses payments or continues charging without your knowledge.

Checking, Savings, and Investment Accounts

Even if the account is solely in your name, your spouse will be able to see how you are depositing, withdrawing, and to whom you are writing checks as well as transferring money.

Post Office Box

Get a post office box so your spouse can't see your mail.

Smart Home and Smart Phones

Don't forget about smart home and phone devices, which can control air-conditioning, the thermostat, alarm systems, wireless cameras, door locks, garage doors, lighting in and outside the home, along with any other properties you might have as well as cloud storage. We have seen this used by one spouse against the other. In one case, the spouse no longer living in the house used the doorbell camera to spy on the other. In another case, the husband, who was ordered to move out of the home, had control of the password for the home's thermostat and would turn off the air-conditioning and turn the heat on during the Florida summer!

IMPORTANT DOCUMENTS TO BE REVISED

Besides changing your passwords, it is imperative to change other documents that affect your legacy, health, and finances.

Last Will and Testament

In one case, John died during the divorce proceedings he had initiated, leaving Sarah, his second wife, the house and the business, where she had worked beside him for many years. During their long-term marriage, his sons from his first marriage had treated her with disrespect and disdain. Although they were also employed by the business, the first thing Sarah did after the funeral and probate of John's will was fire the sons!

Even though a will can be changed during divorce proceedings in Florida, you should get professional advice as to whether this can be done in your state or if you must wait until the divorce is final. States also vary on whether you can entirely cut your spouse out of the will or if they can still get a percentage of the estate. For example, in Florida even if you attempt to disinherit your spouse without your spouse's agreement, the Florida statutes provide for the spouse getting 30% of the estate if death occurs while still married.[3]

Living Will and Advanced Healthcare Directive

If your spouse had been appointed to make healthcare decisions for you, you don't want them in charge of your healthcare while going through the divorce or thereafter.

Power of Attorney

You don't want your spouse to be making decisions over your health or finances.

HIPAA Release of Confidential Medical Records

If you have listed your spouse as being able to see your medical records or as an emergency contact, you may want to change these designations.

Revocable Living Trust

If you have a revocable living trust as part of your estate planning, then revise this document with your attorney or another trusts professional so it reflects your changed circumstances.

Life Insurance

If your spouse is listed as your beneficiary, now is the time to change this designation.

Auto Insurance

This is especially important if your spouse is an alcoholic, a poor driver, or has a history of accidents, as there is always a chance of an accident. Revise your insurance so that they are on a separate policy and the vehicle they drive is only in their name. You want to protect yourself against being liable if there is an accident while they are driving.

In summary, it is critical to revise important documents and pretend like *all* of your accounts online and offline have been hacked—you need to change access to everything. Don't leave it as a surprise!

CHAPTER 2

COMMON MISTAKES MADE IN EMAILING, TEXTING, AND SOCIAL MEDIA

LIKE MIRANDA RIGHTS, ANYTHING YOU SAY, EMAIL, TEXT, OR POST CAN and most definitely will be used against you! Once sent, these communications are unable to be completely erased, and they may be unearthed during the discovery process in your divorce litigation.

TEXTING AND EMAILING

Text messages and emails between the parties have been entered into evidence in establishing alimony, "time-sharing" schedules (referred to as custody or visitation in some jurisdictions), injunctions, relocation, and for property division. So, it is crucial to watch your language when texting, emailing, or leaving a voicemail. Keep texts, emails, and voicemails sanitized—don't threaten, curse, or insult your spouse. Be civil. You need to be aware that your spouse or other interested people know how to push your buttons and may try to get a reaction that can later be used against you in court.

We have seen this tactic frequently used when children are involved. We can't begin to tell how many transcripts of hearings we've read that caused a case to go badly for the offending parent who sent texts or emails using foul language when addressing the other parent. A husband using the C-word when texting his wife does not endear him to the judge. Sadly, many spouses know how to get their soon-to-be exes to respond in anger, and even if there is no cursing, a response sent in anger may make the sender appear unreasonable.

In one case, text messages entered into evidence showed a reticence by the mother to involve the father in raising their children, which negatively affected her in the court's decision.[4] Alternatively, in another case, the collection of emails and text messages entered into evidence were consistent with the mother's testimony that she routinely allowed additional time-sharing beyond the parties' written agreement, despite the fact that the father was demanding and never satisfied with the extra visitation.[5] Some courts require the parties to communicate through apps, like TalkingParents or OurFamilyWizard, that keep a record of the parties' communications regarding their children. With these apps, all calls and messages are recorded, saved, and cannot be altered.[6] Other benefits include a shared calendar, GPS check-ins (to prove a parent failed to show up at the exchange location), and facilitating the sharing of invoices.

Sometimes sending an email or text knowing it will upset your spouse may feel great for the moment but can have serious consequences. For example, Harold took a picture of a sizable check he was required to pay to his soon-to-be ex-wife, and when sending the email stated, "[t]his is the closest you will ever get to this money." His wife showed the email to her lawyer, who showed it to the judge. The judge did not think this antic was funny. Harold was held in contempt. (Contempt is the failure to obey a court order, which can be punishable with a fine or even imprisonment until the person adjudged to be in contempt complies with the order.)[7]

Trying to show up your spouse can also backfire. While Cynthia and her husband, Arthur, were separated, she sent him an email stating that her boyfriend gave her $75,000 to hire the best divorce attorney, he would continue to fund her, and she never had to pay him back. When Cynthia later attempted to get a court order for Arthur to pay her attorney's fees and testified that she borrowed the money from her boyfriend but had to pay him back, Arthur's attorney entered the incriminating emails into evidence. Cynthia lost.

How Should Self-Serving or Nasty Texts Sent by Your Spouse Be Answered, or Should You Respond at All?

A common mistake made by some litigants is not responding at all to self-serving texts or emails sent by their spouse. What they don't realize is that the spouse is building a case against them with these texts or emails, and by not responding, the court will only be aware of one side—the side that sent the texts or emails. Even if the litigant later testifies about the particular matter in court, the judge may think this is a last-minute attempt to overcome the written communications sent in real time, and those texts or emails would likely have more credibility with the court.

Another common mistake is to answer a nasty text or email with a nasty text or email in return or not answer at all. Your response should answer the nasty text or email in a neutral, civil, or even at best a friendly manner, ignoring the nastiness that may be trying to hook you into a response you will later regret sending. That tends to create the impression of you being the more reasonable party, and it may eventually result in your spouse realizing that these nasty texts are not affecting you in the way they hoped, and stopping this line of communication.

Never hit "send" in anger. If at all possible, wait to respond—for fifteen minutes, an hour, or overnight if necessary. Have a trusted friend, family member, or your lawyer read and censor the response prior to sending. This applies doubly in jurisdictions that have approved monitored communication systems like TalkingParents or OurFamilyWizard.

However, if the texts are life-threatening, do not immediately respond, but instead show them to your lawyer, who may seek a restraining order on your behalf against your spouse. You may also want to call the National Domestic Violence Hotline for expert support. The Florida Department of Children and Families Domestic Violence Hotline provides the following warning: "[y]our abuser may monitor your internet use and may be able to view your computer activity. If you have reason to believe that your computer is not secure, you may wish to use a computer in another location to which your abuser does not have access."[8]

Save All Yours and Your Spouse's Texts and Emails

Save not only your texts and emails but your spouse's texts and emails that are sent to you as well. If you are not using a co-parenting app, you can save them on your phone, computer, or separate cloud storage account, like iCloud, if you have one. You can also print them so you have all of them in context. When reading transcripts from divorce trials, we often see one side cherry-picking emails or texts so the messages are out of context, and paint a picture that is damaging to their spouse. That spouse has often not saved the full chain of texts or emails from both parties, and so is unable to put the texts or emails in a proper context which seriously hurts their case.

Common Mistakes Made with Work Emails

You may not be aware that emails sent to your lawyer from your work email address, or emails sent from your lawyer to you at your work email address, may not be protected as being attorney-client privileged (this protects confidential communications between lawyers and their clients relating to seeking or giving legal advice). Sometimes, an employer can access or monitor an employee's email by virtue of the company's policy. There is no expectation of privacy. It is best to check your jurisdiction's laws on this subject.

COSTLY MISTAKES CAN OCCUR WHEN TRYING TO USE SPYWARE

Your computer and cell phone use can be monitored without your knowledge or consent. Spyware can be an app or software that is used to spy on another's activities or track their location. Some spyware programs can even record all the keystrokes made on the device. Global Positioning System (GPS) trackers, like AirTags, are known to be hidden in vehicles, but they can even be placed on items like a purse or cell phone to track your every move.

Installing a spyware program on your spouse's computer or a GPS on their vehicle may be tempting but should not be done. At best, the illegally intercepted communications are generally excluded from being used as evidence at trial,[9] and at worst, you may find that you are charged with a crime.[10] You may also find yourself faced with civil liability.[11] These options can give your spouse additional leverage in settlement negotiations as well as provide an unfavorable view of your case by the judge should your case go to trial.

When marital discord erupted between Beverly and her husband, James, she secretly installed a spyware program called Spector on James's computer. The Spector spyware secretly took snapshots of what appeared on the computer screen, and the frequency of these snapshots allowed Spector to capture and record all chat conversations, instant messages, and emails sent and received in private online chats between James and another woman, as well as websites visited on the computer. When James discovered Beverly's clandestine attempt to monitor and record his conversations with the other woman, he uninstalled the Spector software, and his attorney filed a motion for a temporary injunction, which was granted, to prevent his wife from disclosing the communications. Later, James obtained a permanent injunction against Beverly, which additionally prevented her from engaging in this activity in the future. The trial court also refused to admit evidence of James's computer activities obtained through the spyware Beverly secretly installed on her husband's computer. Beverly appealed the orders entered by the court, and the appellate court affirmed the trial court's decisions.[12]

Check with your attorney for your jurisdiction's position on recording without the other person's knowledge. In Florida, secretly recording another person, like your spouse, is a third degree felony, punishable by up to five years in prison and a $5,000 fine.[13] Another complication if you are prosecuted, in addition to the expense of hiring a criminal attorney to defend you, is that you may be faced with having to decide whether you should invoke the Fifth Amendment against self-incrimination during your divorce proceeding to protect your rights in the criminal case. This, of course, would not put you in the best light during your divorce litigation, particularly when the opposing counsel purposefully asks questions to trap you into pleading the Fifth.

In summary, your best course of action is to refrain from using spyware on your spouse. If you are concerned about being spied upon, eliminate that outcome by checking for spyware on your smart phones, computers, motor vehicles, and anywhere else you think the spyware may have been installed. If you cannot uninstall it yourself, take your device to a professional to remove it and perform a factory reset, or consider using a reputable antivirus or antimalware program to detect and remove spyware. Spyware can monitor your location, so it is important to be careful where you go with your phone or whichever device you think has the spyware. You may want to temporarily use another device, like a computer at a public library or a trusted friend or family member's phone or computer.

SOCIAL MEDIA POSTS AND SOCIAL NETWORKING SITES—A TREASURE TROVE OF INFORMATION

Social media sites can provide a treasure trove of information in divorce proceedings. According to The American Academy of Matrimonial Lawyers, 81% of its members have used or defended against evidence from social networking sites.[14] Posting to a "private" group is still generally treated as voluntarily sharing with the public for evidentiary purposes. Generally, the photographs posted on a social networking site are neither privileged nor protected by any right of privacy, regardless of any privacy settings the user may have established.[15] Social media posts may be discoverable and admitted into evidence if they are relevant and admissible or calculated to lead to the discovery of evidence that is admissible.[16] As we previously pointed out, you can never completely erase your posting history from your computer or other devices, even if you post in "private" or "incognito" mode.

Mistakes to Avoid When Posting on Social Media Sites

We are continually amazed at the social media posts made by litigants during their divorce. It sometimes seems like they lose all common sense when proclaiming to their friends and the immediate world what is presently going on in their lives. We have seen vacation photos by spouses claiming to have no money, and spouses claiming they can't work because of a medical condition or disability but with photos that show them doing intense physical activity. There are photos of money being spent on expensive or frivolous purchases, such as jewelry or luxury automobiles, when in the past, that spouse drove an economy car. There are photos showing a new relationship a spouse is having, which can inflame the other spouse, especially if the photos include the parties' children. There are also obvious inconsistencies that find their way into social media, such as a spouse claiming to no longer have or never have had that Rolex watch or a particular diamond bracelet, and then a new picture on a social media site shows them going to a gala wearing the very piece of jewelry they affirmed under oath had disappeared or never existed. Some spouses want to feel free and party after separating, and their posts are filled with pictures of them looking drunk or using drugs, which can have a negative effect when the parties are fighting about time-sharing/custody with their children. Prior to and early in the litigation, you should review all of your spouse's known social media accounts to which you have access, and download, screenshot, or otherwise copy any relevant content.

The safest path during your divorce is to refrain from posting on social media. If you must continue to post, then block your spouse from your social media accounts. However, this is not always fool-proof as your spouse may be able to obtain the postings from your accounts through friends or even your children, who have access to the accounts.

Including negative or disparaging posts about your spouse on social media can backfire in ways that you may not realize. For example, posting may be seen by friends with access to the sites, who have children attending the same school as your own children, and these posts can become the subject of gossip at school, causing your children unnecessary embarrassment and emotional turmoil.

What happens if you have posts on a social media site that you want to get rid of? Some lawyers have advised to delete posts or even close the account upon filing for divorce. Other lawyers have even told their clients to clean up their social media accounts during the divorce proceedings. However, there are definitely downsides to taking these actions, which can have real financial consequences. Deleting photos and posts is called "spoliation," which is the legal term for the intentional destruction, mutilation, alteration, or concealment of evidence.[17] If proved, spoliation may be used to establish that the evidence was unfavorable to the party who altered or deleted the posts.[18] There may also be monetary sanctions imposed by the court against the offending party.

If strategically appropriate, your counsel may send a letter to the opposing counsel demanding that your spouse not delete or edit any posts, texts, or other social media activity, or your own attorney may have received such a letter. Litigants are permitted to request relevant information from the other party, and many attorneys will engage in this process to find out what was changed or deleted from a site after a certain date, like after the petition seeking a divorce was filed.

In summary, social media can become a minefield during the divorce process. To avoid costly mistakes, the best approach is to refrain from posting.

PROTECT YOUR PHYSICAL WELL-BEING AND SANITY

MANY SPOUSES GOING THROUGH A DIVORCE DO NOT PROTECT THEIR physical well-being and emotional health. They may overeat because of the emotional turmoil they are going through. Others stop eating, some from stress and others because they want to have a new body to go with their soon-to-be newly single status. Some spouses have trouble sleeping and others sleep the day away. However, this is the time to take care of yourself.

Four areas are critical to physical and mental health. They are:

- Exercise
- Nutrition
- Sleep
- Stress management

Exercise is important to your physical health. Consider going to the gym, playing basketball or tennis, swimming laps, or running to get your heart pumping. You can also do other physical exercise, like walking outside, gardening, washing your car, or cleaning your house. Just get moving! Exercise is also important for your mental health as it can ease symptoms of depression, lessen anxiety, and help you to get a better night's sleep.

Nutrition is key. The old adage "you are what you eat" is important during your divorce because the food we eat is crucial for our health and well-being. Now is not the time to fill up on junk food, as tempting as it might be. Eating a balanced diet that includes fruits and vegetables will keep your energy level up, help you to maintain a healthy weight, and improve your mental health and the quality of your sleep.

Getting enough sleep helps you think more clearly, which in turn will help you make better decisions. It has been found that sleep can help in maintaining your weight. It can also help with your immune system to fight off sickness and infection. Most adults need seven or more hours of sleep each night. Try to stay on a regular schedule so you will feel rested when you wake up. If possible, go to bed and wake up at the same time every day. Avoid eating a large meal within a few hours before bedtime, and avoid caffeinated soda, coffee, and tea, as the caffeine in those drinks are a stimulant and can interfere with sleep. Take an hour before bedtime to wind down your day. Avoid intense exercise or artificial light from a television, phone, or computer screen and keep your bedroom cool when it is time to go to sleep.

Stress can be reduced through exercise, a healthy diet, and getting enough sleep. Deep breathing, meditation, and yoga can be effective as well. Making time for hobbies, listening to music, socializing with people you enjoy being with, and just laughing are other ways of reducing stress.

PROTECT YOUR SANITY

Some spouses feel it is a sign of weakness to get professional help. However, the opposite is true. It is best to talk to a therapist or counselor about your feelings, as a professional can assist you in sorting them out. Life coaches can help you develop coping skills and strategies to manage the stress and complex emotions of divorce, as well as help you identify your goals and priorities, empowering you to make decisions for your future. These professionals can provide the support you need during this very emotional time.

You don't want to unload on your divorce attorney. Most lawyers charge by the hour, and your money would be better spent with a healthcare professional. As discussed earlier, you don't want to send any type of communication to your spouse while stressed that could easily haunt your divorce. Vent where it is safe to do so. A therapist or life coach may be able to help you feel in control when dealing with stressful day-to-day situations.

Emily was going through a divorce with a controlling and verbally abusive spouse. She filed for the divorce after a long, unhappy marriage. They had to share occupancy of their home during the divorce proceedings for financial reasons but stayed in separate bedrooms. At night, her husband would bang on Emily's locked bedroom door, demanding that she open it. In the daytime, whenever they were home at the same time, he would stand over her and tell her that she was a fool for wanting to leave their marriage, as no one else would ever want to love her. During the divorce, Emily sought the help of a therapist, who provided support and enabled her to understand how not to react so that her husband realized his actions were no longer having an impact on her. The years of being beaten down by his insults had made her insecure, but she hung in there, trying to remember that these were just words and that she was a person of worth. Emily learned she was in control of her own emotions, attitude, and conduct.

Be aware that there is the tendency of some spouses to engage in emotional spending, whether it be at the mall or from late-night cable shopping sites. Other spouses may gamble to get away from the stress of the divorce, drink to excess, or take drugs. It is important to get the help you need from professionals and have the support of close friends and family, who will be there for you during this stressful time.

You should have a small support group of family and close friends you can talk to about your divorce. However, be mindful that if you constantly talk only about your divorce, it will begin to wear thin on family and friends, even though they may be sympathetic to your present situation. Try not to talk disparagingly about your spouse and air all your "dirty laundry" in an attempt to get them to hate your spouse while supporting you. Should you reconcile with your spouse, you will not be able to take back the negative comments which will color your friends' relationships with both you and your spouse. Family relationships with your spouse may also be permanently damaged.

Be prepared to lose some of your marital friends during and after the divorce. If you are used to dining out with your marital friends, understand that you are no longer part of a couple, so it is not unusual to no longer be included when couples go out to dinner, as they may not want a third wheel. You might be relegated to a luncheon friend. Keeping this in mind may help to lessen the hurt or abandonment you may feel.

Finally, and what may be very difficult for most spouses going through a divorce, is not to think about it 24/7 as this will not reduce your anxiety and will only cause you additional stress.

Another way to reduce your stress is by hiring the right attorney with the knowledge to protect your interests. Having the right attorney can make all the difference in your divorce and your peace of mind. The next chapter provides pointers to help make the right decision for you.

CHAPTER 4

HOW TO PICK YOUR DIVORCE LAWYER

PEOPLE SEEM TO SPEND MORE TIME AND EFFORT DECIDING ON WHICH restaurant to go to than which lawyer to hire! They often wait too long, and as a result, may lose thousands of dollars by accepting an offer made by their spouse without the benefit of having legal counsel and being informed of their rights.

Jerry hired an attorney who prepared a settlement agreement that was totally one-sided in his favor. He told his wife, Cindy, that this was the best she would be able to get from a judge, so she signed it. A little more than a year later, Cindy consulted with a divorce attorney after finding out how difficult it was to live with the terms of the agreement. Unfortunately, at that point in time, there was little the attorney could do for her because she had waived alimony and given up any interest in property she would have likely received. Cindy was also left with excessive debt that she did not realize she would have by signing the settlement agreement. She should have consulted with a divorce attorney at the start of the divorce process.

WHAT YOU NEED TO DO BEFORE YOU HAVE THE INITIAL CONFERENCE WITH A LAWYER

Gather as many financial documents as you can before the consultation. It will streamline the initial consultation and make it more meaningful.

If possible, make a list of your marital assets and liabilities as well as the separate property you and your spouse acquired prior to the marriage. You should also gather financial records like loan applications, financial statements, tax returns, employment records, and bank statements. You want to have as many different records as possible. Couples may exaggerate on loan applications while being more conservative on their tax return. Having a variety of documents will provide a greater opportunity for a more accurate financial picture.

Lastly, and most importantly, documents have a way of disappearing once your spouse becomes aware that you are planning for a divorce. You can save these documents in an account that your spouse has no access to such as opening a Google account if your emails have been in Microsoft, or in a Dropbox account, or a separate iCloud account. You can also make paper copies of these documents which you need to keep in a safe place that your spouse will not know about or find.

You want to get a general idea of your spending. A sample financial affidavit excerpt is included in Chapter 15, which lists many categories that comprise the types of spending in a marriage, the types of debts, and categories of assets and liabilities. You can use this as a guide. You also want to take an inventory of the personal property in your home. Pictures or a video are extremely helpful and can identify property your spouse may later claim does not exist.

You may want to remove your jewelry and your family heirlooms from your home to leave with a relative or trusted friend before filing for divorce. We have often seen these items disappear or be held hostage by the other spouse during the divorce proceedings.

Having all these documents at your disposal will make your initial conference with an attorney much more productive. We have included a list of questions you may want to ask.

Confirming the Lawyer's Experience and Expertise in Divorce Law

- What percent of their practice is family law and divorce?
- Have they received a certification in family law by the State Bar Association? Many states have certification programs that enable lawyers to assert they are specialists in a particular area of the law.

There are also organizations or companies that rate attorneys—some of which lawyers can pay for to get the rating, and others that are truly independent. An attorney with an AV rating from Martindale-Hubbell is a good place to start.[19]

- Is their practice focused on contested divorce or collaborative divorce?
- Do they generally settle or go to court?
- What is their courtroom experience? What is their knowledge and application of the rules of evidence and their skill at cross-examination?
- Do they know the judges they will be before?
- If your spouse has already hired a lawyer, does your potential attorney know your spouse's lawyer and how he or she practices divorce litigation? Is your spouse's attorney reasonable so that your attorney can work with them or will it be an all-out war?
- How long will the divorce take based upon the facts of your case?

How the Lawyer's Office Is Run

- Is the lawyer a sole practitioner, or are there other attorneys who will be working on your case? If so, who are they and what is their experience and expertise?
- If a sole practitioner, does the attorney have support staff, like law clerks, paralegals, or secretaries?
- Who will be your office contact?
- What is their availability and responsiveness? Through the years we have come to know that some attorneys and their staff are available and have effective communication with their clients, while others are very hard to reach or not responsive.
- How do they like to communicate with the client—in-person conferences, Zoom, phone calls, emails, or texts? Do they ask about your preferred method to reach you?
- Does the firm use AI-related software, and if so, to what extent?

- How extensive is their discovery process (the process of finding information about your spouse's assets, liabilities, and other factors that are key to your spouse's case and yours)? Some attorneys will only do the minimum amount of work needed, while others are known to "churn the file," resulting in unnecessary litigation and excessive legal fees. People you know who have used the attorney's services may be able to provide you with additional information about the attorney's litigation practices.

Your Personal Impressions While Interviewing the Lawyer

It is important that you have a comfort level with the lawyer, trust them, and are okay with their general temperament.

- Does the attorney listen to you?
- Does the attorney answer your questions during your initial meeting?
- Does the lawyer speak in "legalese," or are their answers easy to understand?
- Do you feel the lawyer is talking down to you?
- Do you feel you are being rushed?
- Does the attorney provide you with realistic expectations—best- and worst-case scenarios—regarding your case?
- Does the lawyer appear to be empathetic?

Recommendations and Reviews

- What are the lawyer's online reviews?
- Have any friends or family used the lawyer's services, and if so, what is their overall recommendation? One of the biggest complaints we hear from potential appellants is that their trial counsel did not communicate with them, were not responsive, and were very hard to reach.

Legal Fees and Other Costs to the Client

- Is there an initial consultation fee?
- What will be the retainer and cost deposit? The retainer is the legal fee to start the case and once it is used up you may be required to replenish it as well as pay ongoing legal fees and additional costs during the divorce proceedings.
- Are you billed a processing fee if you pay using a credit card?
- What are the expected costs in your litigation? Will experts be needed for business valuation, a forensic accountant to value assets and liabilities, a vocational expert to evaluate you or your spouse's ability to work and the type of jobs that are available, a real estate appraiser, or another type of expert that would be necessary for your case, such as a tax lawyer or a trusts and estate lawyer? There may also be photocopying and printing costs.
- What is the lawyer's general estimate for what the divorce will cost overall?
- Based on the facts of your case, will the lawyer initially attempt to have your spouse pay your fees and costs?
- Does the lawyer's firm bill separately for every email and conversation no matter how short? If there is hourly billing, is the billing done in 6-minute increments? In 15-minute increments? This can make a big difference in the overall fee, as a lawyer with a lower hourly rate can end up charging more than a lawyer with a higher billing rate depending upon how they bill incremented time. For example, a lawyer billing the minimum amount of time in responding to an email then:
    - $400/hr at increments of 1/4 hr, or 15 minutes reviewing the email costs $100.
    - $400/hr at increments of 2/10 hr, or 12 minutes, that email costs $80.
    - $500/hr at increments of 1/10 hr, or 6 minutes, that email costs $50.

Also consider if there are separate incremental charges for reading your email and then sending a response.

Other Methods for Charging Legal Fees.

Some lawyers charge a flat fee to handle the entire case. Others charge a flat fee for certain parts of the case, with an hourly rate to begin thereafter. Unless you have a very simple divorce, beware of flat fees because the lawyer has no incentive to spend the time that may be necessary to properly represent you.

In some states, lawyers can charge on a contingency basis; they get paid a percentage of the award. In Florida, attorneys are not allowed to have a contingency fee agreement in a divorce case. Consider:

- How often are invoices sent?
- Does the lawyer have payment plans?
- Does the lawyer require you to refresh the retainer when it is used up to a certain point, or are you billed for work done without having to keep replenishing the retainer?

MULTIPLE CONSULTATIONS

Many attorneys will advise you to speak with more than one lawyer before making a final choice as they want you to be comfortable with your ultimate choice.

Some lawyers will advise you to consult with possible problem lawyers so that your spouse can't hire them because they are conflicted out. Once the lawyer speaks with you and learns about your case, he or she should not be able to represent your spouse. There are ethics rules that lawyers must follow. In Florida, these are the Rules of Professional Conduct which are enforced by the Florida Bar.

A common mistake that is often made is waiting to retain an attorney until after being served and then rushing to pick someone without being able to do your due diligence. In Florida, the response to the initial petition your spouse serves on you is due 20 days after being served.

This timeframe varies with different jurisdictions, so it is best to start the process of choosing your lawyer sooner rather than later.

ADDITIONAL ADVICE ON CHOOSING YOUR ATTORNEY

Choosing the right attorney for your needs can reduce your anxiety because of having the confidence that your attorney will work to protect your interests and get you your best outcome. However, there is the temptation to take legal advice from relatives, friends, or acquaintances who are not lawyers. Resist that temptation. Follow your lawyer's advice. That is why you hired and are paying them.

Don't go thinking of having an attorney to exact revenge on your spouse. Doing so will cost a significant amount of money in attorney's fees to pay for this litigation and could likely result in remaining enemies for the rest of your lives, not to mention what this can do to any children you have. Moreover, after all this, you may not get the revenge you are seeking.

"Hand-holding" costs clients money, so don't call, email, or text your lawyer for every little thing. Save up your questions for a comprehensive call, email, or text, unless it is an emergency that can't wait. If you want to vent or discuss emotional issues, it is better to do so with a therapist.

When you do hire your lawyer, you want to get the best results possible. In order to get these results, it is essential for you to be up-front and honest with your attorney about all the facts of your case concerning you, your spouse, and your children, if children are involved.

THE IMPORTANCE OF BEING UP-FRONT AND HONEST WITH YOUR LAWYER

ONE OF THE MOST IMPORTANT THINGS YOU CAN DO IS BE OPEN AND honest with your lawyer.

You may have heard about the attorney-client privilege from television or movies when the lawyer tells a client that they can confide in that lawyer because the lawyer cannot reveal the conversation. The attorney-client privilege protects confidential communications between a lawyer and their client that relate to the client's seeking legal advice. This provides you, the client, with the peace of mind that what you say to your lawyer will be kept in the strictest confidence. Some spouses bring a family member or trusted friend to the consultation, as often the spouse will not remember all that is discussed at such an emotional time. However, there is generally no attorney-client privilege when this third person is present.

COMMON MISTAKES WHEN TELLING YOUR LAWYER ABOUT YOUR CASE

Don't try to spin the information about your case. Be up-front and honest. If you try to spin the information, your attorney won't be fully prepared if and when the truth comes out. You don't want your attorney to be blindsided during a hearing or at trial. Never lie to your lawyer.

If your lawyer repeats that lie to the judge, and should the lie be discovered, then your lawyer may very well prioritize salvaging his or her reputation over keeping you as a client. You may also find yourself fired by your attorney.

Our Firm's fee agreement provides in part that the Firm reserves the right to withdraw from the case "if material facts have been misrepresented or undisclosed to the Firm, or if you fail to follow the Firm's advice or cooperate fully." Moreover, if your lawyer, in relying upon false information you have provided, presents the lie to the court and the judge finds out about being lied to, your credibility will be irrevocably damaged and your case will be seriously jeopardized.

For those who think they can get away with lying or failing to reveal assets, some of the more common areas the judges encounter are:

- Lying about finances, including all sources of income as well as all debts.
- Off-the-record jobs, or second or third jobs.
- Hidden assets or offshore accounts.
- Cheating on taxes.
- Arrests or convictions, including driving under the influence (DUI) or while impaired (DWI), restraining orders, and any crimes for which you were arrested, pled no contest, or were convicted.
- Treatment for mental illness or chemical imbalance.

REHABILITATION MAY BE POSSIBLE IF YOUR LAWYER KNOWS THE REAL FACTS

If your lawyer is aware of a possible problem with your case at the start, you both may be able to work out a plan to turn that negative into a positive. For example, you may be worried about custody/visitation/time-sharing with your children because of a drinking or drug problem. Your lawyer may guide you into a rehabilitation program with periodic drug testing during the divorce proceedings so that near the end of the litigation, you will be able to show a successful rehabilitation. You will also have hard evidence to prove you have turned your life around since separating from your spouse. If you lie about your drinking or drug problem, and it later comes out during a court proceeding, the optics won't be favorable to your case, and the results may be drastically different than if you were initially candid with your lawyer.

OTHER COMMON MISTAKES MADE BY NOT BEING CANDID WITH YOUR COUNSEL

So often, clients only talk about themselves or how they feel about their spouse. What they fail to do is provide their lawyer with factual information about their spouse, including both positive and negative facts. Moreover, they do not give their lawyer enough information about their children. It is crucial the lawyer has this information in order to determine where to further investigate, for settlement negotiations, and for use at trial. So often, what a client may not think is really important may actually have great relevance for their case.

Armed with your choice of a lawyer and having provided him or her with detailed information about your case, the next step is to determine how you would like to proceed, be it by mediation, arbitration, collaborative divorce, or contested divorce.

MEDIATION; ARBITRATION; COLLABORATIVE, UNCONTESTED, AND CONTESTED DIVORCES—HOW ARE THEY DIFFERENT?

WHEN CONTEMPLATING A DIVORCE, THERE ARE SEVERAL DIFFERENT WAYS you can proceed to resolve your case. These various processes include mediation, arbitration, collaborative divorce, as well as uncontested and contested divorce. Each type of procedure has benefits and drawbacks that should be evaluated to determine which will work best for you.

MEDIATION

Mediation is conducted by a neutral mediator who may be an attorney experienced in family law or a retired judge. The mediator does not make the final decision but works with the parties to come to a resolution on their own. Depending upon the jurisdiction, the parties may attend with or without their respective attorneys.

Mediations provide an opportunity for creative solutions that are unique to the parties' situation. The parties are free to think "out of the box" and come to an agreement that suits their purposes, as long as they do not violate the law or public policy. Mediation is not an all-or-nothing proposition. The parties can come to a partial agreement that resolves some of the issues while still preserving the ability to litigate the remaining issues in court. Or the parties may be able to come to a full settlement agreement, which gives them control over their results instead of a judge.

The mediation itself is informal when compared to a courtroom setting and trial. If successful, the parties will have reduced litigation fees and costs as well as shortened time for a resolution of their case. However, mediation won't be beneficial and may ultimately seem like a waste of time if the parties do not want to compromise to resolve their issues. Some spouses want to go to court, others are so angry at the other spouse that there is no chance for resolution.

The mediation itself is confidential to encourage settlement, so anything said in mediation cannot later be used in court proceedings, with very limited exceptions.[20] In Florida, a mediation participant is not permitted by statute to disclose any mediation communication to a person other than another mediation participant or a participant's lawyer. This means that if you are unable to come to an agreement, you can't later tell the judge what your spouse offered to settle your case in the mediation, or about any conversations you had during the mediation. Violating confidentiality could result in sanctions by the court, including but not limited to costs, attorney's fees, and mediator's fees. In Florida, parties are required to mediate prior to seeking temporary alimony or child support, as well as mediate prior to the final hearing or trial in their case.

ARBITRATION

Unlike mediation, where the parties can make the ultimate decisions regarding their case, in arbitration, the arbitrator serves as a judge who is responsible for resolving the issues and making the final decision instead of the parties. Arbitration avoids going through the court system, which can be a long, drawn-out process, and may end up being less costly. Arbitrations are generally held in private, which may appeal to those who don't want the details of their finances or other personal issues to be known. There is also more room for flexibility, especially in the timing of the hearings and selection of the arbitrator.

However, a major drawback to arbitration is if you disagree with or are unhappy with the arbitrator's decision. Unlike with trial court decisions, the grounds for vacating the arbitration award are extremely limited. In many jurisdictions, like Florida, the arbitrator is not bound to follow the law.[21] You may find yourself with a determination that runs contrary to the law of your jurisdiction, and yet you have no recourse to appeal on that basis. Basic rules of evidence, which provide protection to litigants, may not apply in your case. Should you decide to arbitrate, it is crucial to get a reputable arbitrator knowledgeable in family law, particularly in dealing with divorces.

COLLABORATIVE DIVORCES

A collaborative divorce is just that—a collaboration between the parties to resolve their divorce as an alternative to fighting it out in court with a judge deciding their case. This process has the best chance of success where couples are engaged in a "friendly" divorce. The parties must be willing to provide an open and honest exchange of information in a confidential setting.

Each spouse hires a collaboratively trained divorce lawyer—a lawyer who has taken special courses in collaborative divorce—and works with a team comprised of a neutral accountant and a mental health expert to facilitate communication, especially where children are involved. The goal is to provide a neutral safe place so the divorcing couple can resolve their issues civilly. A collaborative divorce team may also include real estate brokers, financial advisors, and other knowledgeable professionals to aid in the divorce process.

The drawback to collaborative divorce is if the process breaks down, and the parties are unable to come to a marital settlement agreement, they cannot continue to use their same attorneys if they now will be litigating the case in court. The parties must hire new counsel and start all over. The failure to resolve their issues will now substantially increase the cost of divorce, and the delay in not initially litigating increases the time it will take to resolve their case.

UNCONTESTED AND SIMPLIFIED DIVORCES

An uncontested divorce is different than a collaborative divorce, as usually the parties initially agree on all issues related to their case and enter into a settlement agreement. Florida has a Simplified Dissolution Procedure, a type of uncontested divorce where the parties can obtain a quick divorce if they have no minor children or dependent children together, if neither spouse is seeking alimony, if the parties have agreed on how to divide all their assets and debts in a settlement agreement, and if they are willing to give up their right to a trial and an appeal. Both spouses must sign the joint petition seeking dissolution of their marriage, and both must come to the final hearing.

CONTESTED DIVORCES

This is the stereotypical method of using the court system to resolve a couple's disputes over time-sharing, alimony, equitable distribution of their assets and liabilities, and issues involving their children. Your deposition may be taken. Your attorney will be engaged in discovery on your behalf. There will be various motions, hearings, and a trial. A judge will decide your case.

There may be a temporary hearing to decide who gets temporary occupancy of the house, temporary alimony, and a temporary time-sharing/visitation schedule. Don't be discouraged if you lose some of the hearings; you may learn what is needed to present to the court so you will be successful at the final hearing—at trial. For example, the court may initially award you temporary alimony that is inadequate for your needs. You then obtain the necessary facts, through your forensic accountant, to prove that your needs are much greater and that your spouse has the ability to pay the increased sum. Even though you lost an initial battle, you may ultimately win the war.

However, the same does not always hold true with time-sharing/visitation. The longer the time elapses with the temporary time-sharing/visitation arrangement, especially if the children seem to be adapting, the more likely the judge will decide not to change what appears to be working, so as not to change the status quo at trial.

Unless you are able to reach a settlement of your case, or a partial settlement of some of the issues related to your finances or children, you will need to go to trial where a judge will decide your case. You will no longer have control over the apportionment of your assets and liabilities or the custody and time-sharing of your children. In a contested divorce, the judge, who does not know you, will make the decision that can have a profound impact on your life and your children's lives.

Overall, settling may be your best option, if you are willing to compromise and are able to have a fair and equitable result. This option will save you time, money, emotional headaches, and heartaches, as you will have control over the outcome.

PART 2

MISTAKES TO AVOID DURING YOUR DIVORCE PROCEEDINGS

DOES IT REALLY MATTER WHO FILES FIRST?

YES, IT DOES REALLY MATTER WHO FILES FIRST, AND THIS SHOULD BE ONE of the first discussions with your attorney. Some spouses are nervous about filing first—they don't want their children to think they were the parent who sought to end the marriage.

However, when you file first you set the tempo—your initial filing, called a Petition or Complaint depending upon your jurisdiction, allows you to be the first to inform the court about the issues you intend to raise in your divorce. You also have an advantage at your trial. The party that files first presents their case first and has the ability to make the first impression about the theory of their case by telling their side of the story first. Your spouse may be put on the defensive by having to rebut what has already been presented.

But don't think that just because you get to speak first you will automatically win. The judge will be listening to the testimony and evidence presented by your spouse. However, we have been told by some divorce lawyers that they think a good first witness has the best opportunity to sway the judge. Another advantage of filing first is that you will also have the last word. You have the opportunity to rebut the testimony or other evidence presented by your spouse.

By filing first, you will generally have already obtained critical documents to your case, which may have been gathered prior to your initial meeting with your attorney. As pointed out in Chapter 4, documents that may cast a negative light on your spouse or affect your family's financial picture have a way of disappearing once the case is filed.

Sometimes a spouse will attempt to get a restraining order as a prelude to or along with filing for divorce. This can result in the other spouse being barred from the marital home and their children, as well as initially providing the judge with a negative view of the offending party.

It is important to discuss with your lawyer the benefits and drawbacks of divorce, as well as the best time to file. You should never file impulsively or in anger. Be certain there is no way to make the relationship work. In discussing your case with the attorney, you may realize that divorce does not make sense at that time or that the marriage may still be salvaged with counseling. If that is the case, the parties should seriously consider trying to save the marriage and look at divorce as the last possible option. Once you file, you may not be able to reconcile— your spouse may not want to get back together. If there is the possibility of reconciliation after filing, only the party that filed the Petition or Complaint for divorce can dismiss the case if their spouse has not yet responded to the Petition or Complaint. Since you control whether the case gets dismissed, it may give you an advantage when determining reconciliation.

In other situations, it may be advisable to wait for financial reasons. For example, a bonus may be given during a specific month each year to one of the parties, so it may be advisable to wait until the bonus is received to maximize the amount of income the parties have. In one of our cases, Charlie had a business where his biggest client's receivables were paid twice a year, in June and December. His wife, Arlene, waited until the client paid the invoice before filing. This enabled the parties to have that additional income considered as part of the husband's earnings.

There are spouses who hesitate to file for divorce when experiencing an economic downturn in their finances. Yet, this may be the best time for the spouse paying alimony to file, as the spouse receiving alimony may be awarded less because of the diminished economic circumstances.

Some states have enacted statutes that consider the length of a marriage when determining the type of alimony that can be awarded (for example, if the marriage will be considered a short-term, medium-term, or long-term marriage). Florida recently lengthened short-term marriages from 7 to 10 years, medium-term marriages from 7-17 years to 10-20 years, and long-term marriages from more than 17 years to more than 20 years. If you are on the borderline so that a potential alimony award will be much greater by waiting, then a decision must be made as to whether you should file sooner or later, depending upon the result you are seeking as either the spouse who would be receiving or paying that alimony.

There may be a wedding, bar mitzvah, confirmation, or other important family or close friend's event that is upcoming and the spouse who is considering filing first may want to wait until after that important family occasion.

Your lawyer will also want to discuss the essential jurisdictional requirements for filing. In Florida, there is a six-month residency requirement before you can file for divorce. If married in another country, you can generally get divorced in the United States if you meet the residential requirements. Your lawyer can tell you the residency requirements in your jurisdiction. Some states also have minimum legal waiting periods between your filing date and the date the divorce can be finalized.

Because each case is unique, it is important to discuss your own situation with your attorney so you can make the best decision for when to file.

DRESS AND DECORUM IN THE COURTROOM AND ONLINE HEARINGS

DOES IT REALLY MATTER WHAT I WEAR TO COURT?

First impressions really do matter. Within the first seven seconds of meeting, people will have a solid impression of who you are—and some research suggests a tenth of a second is all it takes to start determining traits like trustworthiness.[22] You will be judged on your looks long before you are judged on your words or actions.

It definitely matters what you wear to court. The judge will take notice of how you choose to present yourself. It is important to understand that dressing appropriately shows respect for the court and that you are taking your divorce seriously. You may think it is obvious what is appropriate to wear to court, but through our years of practicing law, we have learned this is not always the case.

You should dress for the socioeconomic image you want to convey. In many jurisdictions, the judge can consider any asset of the party, whether marital or nonmarital, accumulated before or during the marriage when awarding alimony and child support.

Jerry attended a hearing dressed very moderately and conservatively, claiming he was without funds to pay his temporary alimony arrearage (money he owed but had failed to pay). His dress portrayed this economic circumstance with one exception—his jewelry. Jerry was wearing a gold Rolex watch and a diamond pinky ring, which, of course, contradicted his testimony of being too broke to pay his soon-to-be ex-wife. The judge was not amused, commented on Jerry's jewelry, and told him he had to sell the Rolex and ring to pay the back alimony.

Your dress can have a positive or negative effect in the way a judge may perceive you. There was a case involving two warring spouses concerning their children's time-sharing issues. The husband was dressed conservatively, while the wife wore a tight, low-cut cocktail dress and red, open-toed stilettos. Her attorney, who never had a conversation with her about appropriate dress, was aghast. The case settled just before the hearing was to begin.

If you want a general rule to follow, it is this: Wear conservative dress that reflects your lifestyle. Some attorneys advise to dress like you are going to a job interview. For men, this would mean wearing a suit and tie, a sports coat, or clean and neat clothing. No leisure suits, shorts, T-shirts, or flip-flops. Women should wear a conservative dress, business suit, skirt and blouse, or pants suit. No tube tops, shorts, cocktail dresses, revealing clothes, or flip-flops should be worn.

WHAT BEHAVIOR IS UNACCEPTABLE IN COURT?

Common sense is not so common. We have read trial transcripts where spouses and sometimes even their attorneys are admonished by the judge for rolling their eyes, shaking their heads, and making faces while their spouse or another witness is testifying. So often, these litigants think they are helping their case when shaking their head to show the court that the witness who is testifying is lying, but their actions only end up annoying the judge. You need to be aware of some other behaviors that are a no-no:

- Don't talk out of turn unless instructed by your attorney.
- Don't talk over the judge.
- Don't interrupt anyone while they are talking.
- No shouting, yelling, or cursing in the courtroom or right outside the courtroom.

We know of judges telling a spouse's lawyer, "[i]f you don't get your client under control, I'm going to hold him [or her] in contempt." You definitely don't want to get on the wrong side of the judge who will be deciding your case!

If your attorney is refusing to present evidence you feel is key to your case, have your lawyer ask if you can get a short bathroom break from the court. Before returning to the courtroom, have a discussion with your attorney as to why you think it is important to your case to enter those documents into evidence. Unfortunately, we have had many clients over the years whose trial attorneys didn't present what they believed was key evidence to the court, then bitterly complain about this once they had to appeal the judgment. The client just didn't know what to do at trial.

Other seemingly obvious actions by litigants in the courtroom that annoy judges occur much too often, so remember the following rules:

- Don't chew gum.
- No texting.
- No playing video games.
- Turn off your phone, or at least put it on silent.

Should your hearings take place online, all of the same rules apply just as if you were physically present in the courtroom. Additionally, be somewhere quiet like a private room at home or any empty office. You do not want background noises and distractions interfering with the proceeding. Do not appear for the proceeding on your phone while driving or shopping! Besides the fact that these activities pull your attention away from the court, it conveys to the judge that whatever else you are presently doing is far more important than your legal case.

In other words, pay attention, and look and behave in a professional and mature manner!

THE DOS AND DON'TS FOR SUCCESSFUL DEPOSITIONS AND HEARINGS

STEVEN'S DEPOSITION WAS BEING TAKEN THAT MORNING. HIS ATTORNEY told him there was nothing to worry about. Steven had never prepared for the deposition with his attorney but was assured to just answer the questions that were being asked by his wife's attorney and everything would be fine. But everything was not fine. Steven had trouble answering many of the financial questions being asked about documents his attorney had filed on his behalf. His wife's attorney seemed to know many of the weak points of Steven's case, and Steven did not know what to say to present himself in the best light. He was stumbling over his words, and his answers were inconsistent. The deposition proved to be a disaster. Steven now realized he would be in a much weaker position if he even hoped to settle his divorce case.

However, you can learn from Steven's mistakes. This chapter will help prepare you to have a successful deposition and understand how to navigate being cross-examined at trial.

FORMS OF DISCOVERY DURING YOUR DIVORCE

During the divorce proceedings, the parties want to find out more about the other side's case. The gathering of this information is called discovery. There are four major ways of seeking this information:

interrogatories, requests for production, requests for admission, and depositions.

Interrogatories are written questions that must be answered under oath. Requests for production usually seek documents or other physical evidence from the other party. Requests for admissions are written statements that must be admitted or denied under oath in writing. Then, there are depositions.

A deposition generally occurs during the discovery phase of the divorce, when the parties are trying to find out more about each other's case. A lawyer will ask the deponent (the person whose deposition is being taken) a series of questions that the person is required to answer orally under oath, while a court reporter or some other authorized person or officer of the court takes down stenographically or by a recording device, everything that is said. The deposition usually takes place in an attorney's office or conference room. Sometimes a videographer may be hired to record the deposition, so there will be both a visual and written recording of the deposition, once it is transcribed by the court reporter.

THE PURPOSE OF YOUR DEPOSITION

The purpose of your deposition is threefold. First, your spouse wants to discover as much as he or she can about your case. Second, the deposition will lock in your testimony. Your spouse's attorney will be looking for any inconsistencies so you can be impeached (the legal term for discrediting you to persuade the judge you are not being truthful). Third, the deposition will aid opposing counsel in sizing you up as a witness to see how you handle yourself while being cross-examined, and to determine if you are likeable, believable, and knowledgeable about the subject matter you will be testifying about.

Most family law cases involve issues of fact, so your credibility or the credibility of your witnesses can make or break your case at trial and can also affect settlement negotiations. An important way of enhancing your credibility or the credibility of your witnesses is to have your lawyer prepare or "prep" you before your deposition is taken and again before any important hearing where you will be testifying.

Your preparation for a deposition and for a trial are very similar, though there are some differences in the format. In a deposition, your attorney can make an objection to a question that is asked, but the deponent must still answer the questions, with a few exceptions.[23] At trial, if a question is asked that your attorney believes is objectionable, he or she will object and should state the legal reason for the objection. It will then be up to the judge to decide whether you will be required to answer the question.

At your deposition or trial, how you present yourself is key. You should respond to questions in a straightforward manner without sounding evasive. You can't be hemming and hawing, rolling your eyes upward, or stumbling over your answers. You also don't want to sound rehearsed; your answers should instead be smooth and consistent— almost off-the-cuff. That is why prepping for your deposition or an important hearing is absolutely necessary. Otherwise, you are flirting with disaster.

We've lost count of the number of deposition and trial transcripts we have read where it is apparent the deponent or witness was not adequately prepared. This type of prep takes time to do it properly. So often when we talk to clients who have lost at trial, we learn they had no witness prep or a very short prep of maybe a half hour or hour before their deposition was taken or they went to trial. Prepping the witness can be an all-day affair, and in some cases, take more than a day, depending on the complexity of the case.

WHAT YOU SHOULD DO TO PREPARE

First, you and your attorney should discuss a game plan regarding what you are trying to accomplish in your divorce and what results you think your spouse wants.

Next, go over all the major court filings. So often we have reviewed transcripts where the deponent is asked a question about their initial petition/complaint or discovery that they had signed (like interrogatories or requests for admissions), and they have no idea about the content of those documents or even what they are for. It is really important to review all pertinent financial documents in your case and understand them and their purpose. This includes not only your responses to discovery, but your tax returns, loan applications, financial statements, checking and credit card statements, your financial affidavit, and any other pertinent document that may be of interest in your case. You may be asked by your spouse's attorney if you are seeking this or that or why you are seeking this or that and you must be able to answer these questions. Know your documents!

It is really important to review the issues to be raised and to anticipate the types of questions to be asked by opposing counsel with your lawyer so you are fully prepared with answers that are consistent with your position. Some clues will be from the discovery previously requested, from the documents you are requested to bring to the deposition, and from exhibits that are listed by either spouse in court filings, especially the final exhibit list for trial. Be especially prepared to answer questions about the initial petition or complaint for dissolution of marriage if you are the Petitioner/Plaintiff, or the counter-petition or counterclaim if you are the Respondent/Defendant, and about your financial affidavit. So often we read transcripts where the spouse does not have a clue about a filing that he or she signed and attested to as true and correct under penalties of law.

During her deposition, Harriet was questioned about her answers to interrogatories regarding trips she had taken since she separated from her husband. Her husband's attorney wanted to know what each trip cost her, in an attempt to show if she had plenty of funds to take vacations, she did not need as much financial support from him. Since her attorneys had thoroughly prepared her, Harriet was able to explain that some girlfriends had paid for her airfare, she stayed with other friends during the trips, and pointed out her credit card statements reflected the minimal amount of money that was spent in fast food restaurants and for the few items purchased during the trips.

It is very important for your financial affidavits to be accurate and to correct them well in advance of trial and of your deposition, if possible. You must also know about all of the items listed in your affidavit and be able to testify to any inconsistencies in your spending. For example, Sally listed spending $2,000 a month on vacations on her financial affidavit. However, it was brought out in the lifestyle analysis by the forensic accountant that she was spending only $500 a month on vacations, leaving a $1,500 monthly difference amounting to $18,000 a year. A witness who is not properly prepped might hem and haw, losing credibility. But Sally, having been fully prepared, responded that her husband was supposed to pay all the children's $36,000 tuition, but he only paid half, so she temporarily refrained from taking her normal vacation to pay the other $18,000 owed to the school. Sally retained her credibility while at the same time, diminishing her husband's position.

When there are real problems or weaknesses in your case, you have to make sure you know how to get in front of them if they are fixable. If not fixable and you can't get in front of them, then you may have to get them buried down deep. However, discuss with your lawyer to have a fallback plan to get around the problem should the other side discover that buried problem or weakness. Otherwise, your credibility will most likely be shot.

When we review the court record, including the transcripts, we often see the client's story is inconsistent or incoherent. Your deposition or trial testimony should tell a story as a coherent narrative that is 100% truthful. Keeping to a truthful storyline is essential because inconsistencies will hurt your case.

Some lawyers role-play with questions and potential answers that they will give to their client. Others will role-play with questions and have the client answer multiple times until the client has a comfort level with that topic. Others just generally cover the topic because they don't want that client to sound rehearsed.

One thing our firm has done when prepping a client is to jump around from topic to topic (like filming a movie, which is not always filmed in sequence). We want the client to be able to keep that coherent narrative and not be inconsistent when answering the questions. Jumping around only to later re-ask the question in the same or in a different way is a technique used by some attorneys to obtain inconsistent answers.

If English is not your native language, you may want your attorney to have a foreign language translator present at your deposition, and if possible, from the same region that you are from. As an example, a French-Canadian client might feel more comfortable with an interpreter who speaks with a French-Canadian dialect and knows how a French-Canadian person would view certain English words or colloquial expressions differently than an interpreter who merely spoke generic French. We have had clients retaining our firm to handle their appeals who lost a significant amount of money they would have been entitled to because they did not understand the meaning of an English word or phrase that had a very different meaning in their native language. Had they had an interpreter at trial, the result might very well have been different.

ON THE DAY OF YOUR DEPOSITION OR HEARING, BEFORE IT BEGINS

Be rested. Try to have a good night's sleep. Eat before the deposition or hearing so you are not hungry while you are being questioned. Take no drugs except for necessary prescribed medications and don't drink any alcohol. You want to be alert.

Wear appropriate clothing to the deposition—the same as you would to court for the financial picture you want to portray (as discussed in

Chapter 8). Also remember, especially if you are being videotaped, to practice proper decorum. We once read a transcript where the deponent, who was being videotaped, was doing her nails while being questioned! During the deposition, the court reporter transcribed her attorney telling her to cut it out. Common sense did not prevail that day!

HOW SHOULD YOU ANSWER QUESTIONS DURING YOUR DEPOSITION OR AT A HEARING?

Speak slowly and clearly, with short, direct, and truthful answers. This is difficult for most deponents to master, including many lawyers whose depositions have been taken! If you ramble on with the answer, you may inadvertently open up a whole new line of questions you did not expect and were not prepared for. If you can give a "yes" or "no" answer, do so instead of a longer explanation.

Example of the wrong way to answer:
Q: Do you own a car?
A: Yes, a brand-new white Mercedes that I bought after we separated.

Example of the right way to answer:
Q: Do you o
wn a car?
A: Yes.

Although you don't want to go off on a tangent, if a question is asked for which a yes or no won't suffice during a court hearing, make sure that before you answer, you tell the judge that the question needs an explanation. This usually occurs when the opposing attorney asks you a leading question framed to give your spouse's version of the facts. When this occurs, you should respond that you can't answer the question with a simple "yes" or "no" because, to be accurate, the answer needs further explanation. Sometimes the court will allow you to expound upon the "yes" or "no" answer, and sometimes the court will say your attorney can clarify this when it's your attorney's turn to question you. Similarly, should a more complete answer be necessary at a deposition and the attorney questioning you will not allow you to say more than yes or no even though you have asked to give a more complete answer, you should plan ahead of time for your attorney to note this exchange and ask you to explain your answer when it is time for your attorney to ask you questions.

Avoid exaggerations or overstatements. Also avoid absolutes like "I never" or "I always." Very few situations call for these extremes, and you can find yourself in trouble when the lawyer questioning you follows up with a situation that makes you appear to be inconsistent, or worse, to appear as if you were lying.

Know the difference between "I don't know" and "I don't recall." "I don't know" implies you don't have any knowledge about that, while "I don't recall" implies you may have known about that but can't retrieve the information at the moment the question is asked. When in doubt, answer, "I don't recall," rather than, "I don't know." If it is later found that you did have knowledge about the thing that was asked but you had answered, "I don't know," in your deposition or at an earlier hearing, then your spouse's attorney can use your answer to show the court you were lying. If you just don't recall, then your lawyer can use a writing or other appropriate matter to refresh your recollection.

If you don't understand the question, say you don't understand it and ask the attorney to repeat the question. If you still don't understand, the attorney may ask the question in a different way.

Never speculate or guess. However, one way to shut down a question is to respond by using any form of the word "speculate," like saying, "I can't answer that question because I would be speculating." Judges don't want a witness to speculate because it doesn't prove anything. Speculation adds no probative value to a case.

Don't anticipate attorney's questions—listen to them before engaging. Many deponents rush with an answer when being questioned. Take your time before answering. You want to make sure you fully understand the question. Also, it gives your attorney the time to object to an improper question.

Be aware that some attorneys will pause between questions. Many people feel uncomfortable with the silence and will break that silence by more fully answering the question and saying more than they should. Don't fall into this trap!

Don't argue with the attorney asking you questions. Don't lose your temper. Try to remain calm because doing otherwise may affect your credibility.

Lastly, keep it real. In a trial where the wife was overly dramatic, it was so obvious she was acting that even the judge remarked about her "crocodile tears." This wife did not get the judge's sympathy she was hoping for. Instead, her performance resulted in the opposite reaction.

DECIDING WHETHER TO READ OR WAIVE READING YOUR DEPOSITION

At the end of your deposition, you are usually given the choice of whether you want to read or waive reading your deposition (either or both parties can request that it be transcribed). We generally recommend reading the deposition because you may see mistakes you made while testifying or mistakes made by the court reporter in transcribing your testimony.

You can make corrections to your testimony on what is called an "errata sheet," which is normally provided by the court reporter along with a copy of the transcribed deposition. Sometimes the court reporter makes an error in taking down the testimony. For example, the reporter may have omitted the word "not" from an answer, which would totally change the meaning of that testimony. This sheet is also the place to expound on the answers to the questions that you were not permitted to testify to with more than a simple yes or no, as well as to make changes to the substance of your answers. In Florida, the deponent is required to state the reason for each change in their testimony.[24]

Once the corrections are made, signed by the deponent, and returned to the court reporter within a reasonable length of time, the court reporter will attach the original errata sheet to the original transcript. The original is then provided to the attorney who requested the deposition be transcribed, as they are initially responsible for paying for the transcription. Later on, the parties can fight about who ultimately pays for these services.

CROSS-EXAMINATION AT HEARINGS OR AT TRIAL

You should also be rigorously prepped for important hearings and trial. When you are called to testify, usually your attorney will have the opportunity to question you first, called direct examination, and will seek to present you in the best possible light. Often, your attorney will cover some of your weak points so that you will have the opportunity to explain them first and soften the potential damage to your case.

After your attorney finishes questioning you, your spouse's lawyer will begin cross-examination. The primary goal in a cross-examination is to discredit the witness. In Florida, a lawyer can ask a witness leading questions over matters covered during direct examination. This means the questions won't be open-ended; and as pointed out earlier in this chapter, many of the questions will be phrased to reflect your spouse's version of the events and require only a "yes" or "no" response.

Your credibility is what the lawyer seeks to damage, so you should be aware of various tactics that are used in an attempt to discredit you. One way is to use your deposition to impeach you if your testimony at trial is inconsistent with something you said during your deposition. The lawyer will read a portion of your deposition testimony to the judge that contradicts what you have just testified to in court. That is why it is so important to keep a consistent storyline throughout your case. Just like you have a storyline, your spouse has their storyline, and your spouse's lawyer will attempt to use your cross-examination to redefine your story so it fits within their version of the facts or events. The lawyer will be looking for the weaknesses of your case and may pepper you with questions where you are most vulnerable. Careful preparation for the hearing or trial should go a long way to helping you best respond to the questions.

One more point: do not use foul language or lose your temper during your cross-examination. This may be difficult, especially if the questions are designed to anger and get a rise out of you. Keep your cool! Let your spouse's lawyer come off as "the bad guy" while you keep your credibility intact.

IN SUMMARY

It should be evident how important it is to properly and fully prepare for your deposition. By doing so, you strengthen your settlement negotiations. You also persuade your spouse and their attorney that you will be a strong, credible advocate for your case if it cannot be settled before trial. If you have to go to trial, being fully prepared will increase your ability to keep your credibility intact during cross-examination, so that you have the greatest chance of having a successful result.

IF A COURT REPORTER DIDN'T TRANSCRIBE IT, IT DIDN'T HAPPEN!

WE ARE CONTINUALLY AMAZED AT THE SPOUSES WHO COME TO OUR FIRM seeking to appeal an order or judgment, only for us to find out there was no court reporter present at trial or at a significant hearing. Through the years, we have spoken to many potential clients who tell us about the errors they believe were made at their trial and the bad rulings by the judge that cost them a substantial amount of money or that caused them to lose significant issues relating to their children. We then have the unpleasant task of explaining to them that they really have no chance to win an appeal because of their mistake in not having a court reporter at that crucial hearing.

Although not in the context of a divorce, a scene in the movie *My Cousin Vinny* provides an example of why it could have been important to have a court reporter at that trial. Near the end of the movie, the prosecutor wants to have a surprise expert witness testify that the tire marks on the road could have only been made by the defendants' car. Vinny objects to having the surprise witness testify, and his objection clearly and concisely provides the appropriate reasons for disallowing this testimony. However, the judge overrules the objection, and allows the expert to testify on behalf of the prosecution, as his testimony was expected to clinch their case. Had the defendants been found guilty, the transcription of the judge's ruling on the objection would have provided an exceedingly strong basis to have overturned the verdict. However, without a court reporter present, there would be no transcribed record that a contemporaneous objection was made nor the exact wording of the objection. It was as if it never happened!

There are three essential reasons for having a court reporter present for important hearings, as the transcription of the hearing can be used:

1. For an accurate record of the court proceedings;
2. To impeach the credibility of witnesses at later hearings or at their deposition;
3. For an appeal.

A divorce attorney will occasionally tell us their client did not want to pay to have a court reporter attend an important hearing during the litigation and sometimes even the divorce trial. However, you should always have a court reporter present for any hearing you or your lawyer think might end up being consequential, and especially for the final hearing. In Florida, only an appearance fee must be paid for the court reporter to attend a hearing. You and your lawyer can later decide if you want the hearing transcribed. The much greater cost is for a transcription of the hearing.

Some jurisdictions provide a way to preserve testimony without independently hiring a court reporter. In these instances, the court has its own in-house court reporting service, or the court provides for a recording to be made during the hearing at no expense to the litigants. Should they desire to have a copy of the recording, they can order it from the appropriate office in the courthouse. Some jurisdictions will be able to transcribe it for a fee, others will require the party requesting a copy to have it independently transcribed by an authorized transcriptionist or court reporter. In Florida, for example, the courts generally record proceedings for domestic violence injunctions.

Family law cases are fact intensive—there is normally a lot of "he said, she said," so transcripts are an essential part of the appellate record. Without transcripts of the trial and other important hearings, you run the risk of the appellate court not being able to properly and fully review your case, so your chances of winning an appeal become exceedingly slim.[25]

THE DOS AND DON'TS OF PARENTING DURING DIVORCE PROCEEDINGS

IF YOU HAVE CHILDREN, THEY SHOULD BE YOUR TOP PRIORITY. PERIOD.

Staying together for the sake of children sounds noble, but it is a terrible idea when there is too much marital tension and the children witness almost constant fighting going on between you and your spouse; all that conflict is destructive. As bad as it sounds, divorce may be the better solution compared to leaving your children in the middle of that awful situation.

When most people think of custody, they think of where the children will be living. This is physical custody. There is also legal custody, which concerns who will make the decisions regarding the children's education, medical care, extracurricular activities, and religious upbringing when the parents are at an impasse regarding these important areas of the children's lives. In Florida, the term "custody" is no longer used; instead, "time-sharing" is used so neither parent is deemed to have "primary" physical custody. Florida's state legislature wanted to end the stigma of one parent merely having visitation. Similarly, parental responsibility or authority have replaced legal custody.

In Florida, there are twenty statutory factors the judge considers when making the decisions on time-sharing and parental responsibility in determining the best interest of the children.[26] Other jurisdictions may have similar factors for best interest considerations or use a different process. Knowing what you should or should not do will enhance your position in the divorce litigation and, more importantly, protect your children's mental health.

Should you and your spouse decide to divorce, be straightforward in telling the children the marriage is ending and you are getting a divorce. Tell them it is not their fault, both of you love them very much, and you won't stop loving them because there's a divorce. If possible, tell the children together with your spouse. But beyond that, try to keep the children out of the divorce as much as possible by refusing to share the daily details about the divorce itself. Intentionally telling children what is going on in the litigation is usually perceived as a means to use your children as weapons in the divorce rather than looking out for your children's best interests. We have seen situations concerning parents who involved their children in spying on the other spouse and enlisted their help in a scheme to have a private detective take pictures to try to gain an advantage in the case. One father actually admitted in his deposition that he got the children involved in the litigation because the case was all about them.

It can even be problematic when children merely overhear what is being said. Children can repeat what they have heard Mommy or Daddy say about the divorce litigation to the other parent or to a third party. This can be especially damaging to the case of the parent carelessly sharing divorce details if the children repeat this information to somebody who ends up preparing a report for the court or testifying as a witness.

Unfortunately, we too often see parents sabotaging the relationship the children have with the other parent. Take the case of Tiffany. This child's birthday was on a weekend during her mother's time-sharing. Tiffany very much wanted to celebrate the occasion with both parents, and her mother told Tiffany she had invited the child's father, who was going to come early to the party to spend additional time with her. The party was scheduled for 11:30 a.m., with lunch to be served at noon. Tiffany got a new outfit for the party and was excited that both her mom and dad would be there. However, her mother told her father the party started at 5:00 p.m. On the day of the party, Tiffany eagerly waited, and waited, and waited for her father, who not only didn't come early, but was entirely absent from the birthday party. Her mother told Tiffany that her father didn't love her or care enough to show up. Of course, when her father came at 5:00 p.m., Tiffany was so upset she didn't want to see him. Tiffany's father was then put in the awkward position of deciding whether to do nothing or to throw her mother under the bus by telling Tiffany what had actually happened and forcing the child to decide whom to believe—which could result in having trust issues with both parents.

One mother was being interviewed by a social investigator, when the child, who was at her father's home for time-sharing, called the mother crying that the father had taken the child's phone away as punishment for misbehaving at an after-school event at their church. The mother put the call on speaker to let the social investigator hear the full conversation. The mother thought she was being clever for doing so. During the call, the mother first commiserated with the child, telling her how the father was unfair, and then counseled the child to just hide the phone from the father next time. When the conversation ended, the mother seemed very satisfied with the way she handled the situation. She didn't realize that besides disparaging the father, she had taught the child it was okay to disregard the father's rules and be deceitful. This incident became a negative factor against the mother in the social investigator's report.

Sometimes, one spouse will try to scare or bully the other by telling them that if they proceed with the divorce, they will never see the children. In many states, that threat has no merit except in the most extreme cases, like when there is clear child abuse or a drug problem putting the children at risk. Even then, judges will generally give some time-sharing/visitation, even if supervised by a third party. The court will be considering the best interests of the child in making the decision.

Don't bad-mouth, denigrate, or talk disrespectfully about your spouse in front of others, especially in front of your children. For example, you shouldn't tell your children that your spouse has had or is having an affair or that you have no money because you are spending it on litigation expenses fueled by the other parent. Blaming the other parent for ending the marriage causes unnecessary turmoil for your children. Most children love both parents and don't want to hear that. Ask yourself if you love your children more than you hate your spouse as your children will ultimately pay that price.

We have read transcripts where fathers have called the mothers the C-word or worse in front of the children, and mothers telling the children their father is lazy, selfish, and useless. This does not play well in court hearings. You should want to allow your children to love both parents without choosing sides.

You should also not actively encourage the children to dislike the other parent's new girlfriend/boyfriend, so the children feel disloyal for liking that person. Again, for your children's benefit, put aside your own feelings.

It is important to act upon your children's needs as opposed to your own needs and desires. Don't fall apart in front of your children. You need to comfort them, not the other way around. Be the adult by putting the children first and diminishing any of their anguish. Avoid burdening children with adult responsibilities; you don't want to rob them of their childhood. Similarly, children need security, so don't tell them about your finances. A child does not need to hear about being unable go to camp because the other spouse has not paid a share of the expenses or that some other need is being unmet due to the cost of now maintaining two households. Try to view the divorce from your children's perspectives and don't make your children choose or feel guilty for loving the other parent.

Additionally, your children should not be used as a go-between for you and your spouse. Communicate directly with your spouse through whatever means you have agreed to or the court ordered, such as TalkingParents or OurFamilyWizard, which can preserve your messages with each other, and are particularly useful in high-conflict divorces. Don't interrogate your children after they have been with the other parent, wanting to know everything they did, what they ate, and who was there. It puts the children in a very uncomfortable position.

Judges look for parents who are flexible with the time-sharing/visitation schedule when the occasion calls for it (for example, picking the child up from school and changing dates to accommodate the other spouse when need arises). Still, if your spouse is not adhering to the schedule by keeping your children from you with excuse after excuse when it is your turn, you can go to the judge and seek contempt against your spouse for being in noncompliance with a court-ordered schedule. Maintain a diary or calendar of when and why you are refused access to use as evidence.

In Florida, a spouse refusing to pay court-ordered child support is not a legal reason to deny that spouse's access to the child for time-sharing/visitation. The flip side of that coin, in Florida, is you cannot legally stop paying child support because your spouse is preventing you from seeing your child. The appropriate remedy is having your lawyer seek the imposition of a contempt order.

Be aggressive in demanding your allotted/ordered time and don't rely on the other spouse saying you can see the kids anytime. Unless your local jurisdiction provides otherwise, until you have a court order, there is no formal, enforceable means of ensuring time with your children. You also need to use the time allotted, because failure to use it is grounds for permanently losing that time down the line.

You may want to seek a quick trial date in the early stages of the dissolution if you are not getting the temporary time-sharing/visitation arrangement you want because the earlier the trial date, the less time there is for everyone to get used to the temporary arrangement. If too much time goes by, the court may keep the status quo as the permanent arrangement.

A not-so-unusual situation we have seen over the years is children refusing visitation/time-sharing with a parent. In these cases, the court-ordered provisions are key to determining whether a parent will be held in contempt for the children's behavior. Orders should clearly set forth the visitation/time-sharing schedule and what is expected of the parents so the schedule is adhered to.

Although generally the better practice, it is not always essential to have the order spell out the conduct required for contempt, but this normally requires a finding of intentional conduct or active interference against the children visiting the other parent.[27] In one case, Sandrine, the mother, was a French citizen living in France, and Brendan, the father, was a United States citizen living in Florida. Their then nine-year-old, who had dual citizenship, lived with Brendan during the school year, and spent spring break and summer vacation with Sandrine, while rotating visitation/time-sharing for Thanksgiving and Christmas. After the child's visitation with Sandrine concluded, Sandrine would take her daughter to the French airport. The child's father flew to that airport just to pick up his daughter for the exchange so they could fly back to the United States together. One time, however, the child refused to leave her mother to go with Brendan and the transfer did not occur. Unfortunately, the custody order did not contemplate how the parties should respond.

Brendan filed a motion for contempt, and at the hearing, the judge found Sandrine had physically prevented Brendan from picking up the child at the French airport and taking her back to the United States with him when the child refused to go. The judge also found Brendan's girlfriend, who had accompanied him to the airport, tried to convince the child to calmly board the plane, but Sandrine rebuked the girlfriend, telling her to stop talking to the child and leave the child alone. The determinative factor that led to Sandrine being held in contempt for willful noncompliance with the custody order was when she physically and intentionally prevented their child from boarding the airplane with Brendan and prevented his girlfriend from assisting.

Sandrine's attorney argued the judge wrongfully held Sandrine in contempt because the custody order did not explicitly delineate the conduct expected of the parties if the child refused to board the plane. That argument might have otherwise worked, but in upholding the trial judge's decision, the appellate court explained that Sandrine did not simply refuse to physically force the child to board the plane, she actively interfered with Brendan and his girlfriend's attempts to retrieve the upset child for visitation. The appellate court concluded that although Sandrine may have initially made the child available, she ultimately prevented the return of the child to her father in direct violation of the custody order.

If a child refuses to go to the other parent's house, a solution may be to have the child go to therapy. There are reunification therapists who are trained in exactly this type of therapy.[28]

Children need as much normalcy as possible and a stable environment generally better meets this need. Without a stable environment, there is a greater likelihood that the judge will limit your time-sharing/visitation with your children.

It cannot be overemphasized that, at a minimum, you need to know the names of your children's friends and how often they see them, their teachers' names, your children's favorite and least favorite subjects, their doctors and dentists or any specialists they see, their daily routine, their extracurricular activities (and show that you have been attending them), as well as their favorite colors, toys, games, and preferred social media. Judges can consider who will take the children to school, extracurricular events, doctor's appointments, and other responsibilities affecting the children in determining time-sharing/custody, as well as determining ultimate parental decision-making authority for the children's education, medical needs, and extracurricular activities.

The judge will be interested in knowing who customarily took the children to school and to medical appointments, who attended school conferences and the children's extracurricular activities. Was either parent a school volunteer or coach of a team the children were on? Which parent shopped, cooked dinner, helped with homework? Which parent was the disciplinarian, and what was the type of discipline imposed? How much quality time was spent with each child? Were the children in daycare? Were babysitters, nannies, or other family members like a grandparent or an older child used extensively for a parent who was working or going out to party? You will also want the judge to know what particular parenting tasks you have performed since separation from your spouse. Sometimes a parent will substantially increase or decrease their participation after separation from their spouse or during the divorce litigation.

We have seen fathers and mothers with very different parenting styles, which causes the children to contend with different rules to conform to or rebel against. If possible, try to agree on and have a united front on such basics as the children's bedtime, homework, and whether and when they can have a phone. But, so long as the parenting seems reasonable, parents can separately have different parenting styles. Still, some parents try to win temporary favor with their children, by buying them presents, or letting them get away with not doing their household chores or keeping their room clean. This can lead to undermining discipline and allowing the children to play one parent against the other. Buying off or bribing the children during litigation can and has backfired. We have seen this when reading the reports of the social investigator or guardian ad litem, who recognize what is occurring after a home visit and discussion with the parties' children and react negatively to this situation in their reports to the court.[29] These behavioral changes in children can also be noted by teachers, school counselors, family friends, and other adults the children regularly interact with, all of whom can be called as witnesses to testify.

You should keep your spouse informed of the children's teachers, school activities, medical care providers, and you should agree, if possible, on educational and medical decisions. Judges like when parents cooperate and communicate with each other. The opposite is also true; you will not make a favorable impression on the judge if you register your children for school and omit your spouse on the list of approved contacts. It doesn't go over well when a mother or father needs to get a court order to attend parent-teacher conferences due to the other parent's interference. You should also refrain from withholding from your spouse information about medical appointments and doctor's or hospital visits. You don't want to sign your children up for an extracurricular activity that purposefully imposes on your spouse's time-sharing/visitation, without first consulting them. In many jurisdictions, this can readily lead to a court-ordered loss of decision-making authority for educational, medical, and/or extracurricular activities for the children.

Consider the impact of travel times for the children when commuting between the parents' homes, as well as to and from school. For example, if one parent lives minutes away from the children's school and the other parent's residence has an hour-long commute each way, that will likely factor into the court's decision for the time-sharing/visitation schedule. Similarly, should one parent purposefully pick an address that will make it very difficult for the children to pursue a favorite extracurricular activity, the court may well consider this. The greater the disparity between what one parent can reasonably do based on where that parent lives versus the impact on the children's day-to-day life determined by the other parent's location is going to matter. When considering school boundaries, the best interests of the children should trump the parents' interests.

Judges can consider if a parent suffers from mental illness or is so disabled they cannot properly care for their children. Judges can also consider the parents' drug or alcohol issues, as well as if there is a criminal record (and the type of crime involved).

However, as pointed out in Chapter 5, a spouse can alter the court's perception of their problem by being forthright and seeking to overcome their issues. Janice was an alcoholic and concerned that her out-of-control drinking would result in limited or supervised visitation with the children, as her husband sought sole custody or at most for her to have limited supervised visitation. Instead of trying to hide or refusing to admit her addiction, Janice joined Alcoholics Anonymous, had regular urine and hair samples taken randomly, which showed her to be clean, and sought additional counseling to deal with her alcoholism. By the time the case went to trial, Janice was able to document being sober for almost a year. The court awarded fifty-fifty time-sharing/custody of the children between Janice and her now ex-husband.

We have seen situations of parents who are caught attempting to provide false evidence regarding their spouse, and when found out, their credibility was destroyed. In one case, Sherry attempted to portray her alcoholic spouse as a dangerous drunk, although he had been clean and sober during the custody fight. After they separated, one early morning, Sherry snuck over to her spouse's home and dumped empty liquor bottles into his curbside recycling bin on a day the child was time-sharing, just before a personal investigator she hired came on the scene to take pictures of the spouse's bottle-filled bin.

In another case, a husband sought to portray his wife as a drug addict. He doctored photographs of her sitting on a couch to look like there were thick lines of cocaine on the cocktail table and a *Scarface*-inspired white cocaine nose and mustache on his wife. Unfortunately for the husband, the judge had spent several years presiding in drug court, as well as on the felony criminal bench. The judge's remarks toward the husband were scathing, with the judge acknowledging the images were faked and were being completely discounted. Moreover, the judge also let the husband know his attempt to mislead the court would bear on the judge's opinion of the husband as a parent. Of course, the wife prevailed in that case.

Courts have taken into consideration where one spouse has sought and received a restraining order against the other spouse for domestic violence. This provides some protection for the spouse and children, since the offending parent may be restrained from coming near the home, must turn in all firearms to the police, and may include other restrictions depending upon the facts of the case. Resist the temptation to proactively seek restraining orders as a litigation strategy to bias the judge. If exposed, the results tend to end very badly for the offending parent, and regardless, the children almost always suffer significant collateral damage.

Worse, we have seen parents raise allegations of sexual misconduct about the other spouse or family members against a child. The police, Department of Children's Services, or a similar agency may be called to investigate. Sometimes the child is coached to express allegations, and this will cause real emotional damage to the child and the other person.

We are not downplaying the very serious nature of sexual abuse. However, you need to be very careful if you intend to raise this issue during your divorce. You need to be sure there is actual sexual abuse, not just indulging in suspicion enhanced by whatever reasons and emotions are being prompted in the middle of divorce. In the event there is a real possibility abuse is occurring, then do whatever is necessary to protect your children while being aware of the upcoming trauma or harmful effects an investigation will cause the children, as there will be multiple interviews and invasive physical examinations.

There are far more mundane types of protection to consider as well. If your children have allergies, make sure not to expose your children to them, whether that is by preventing pet dander, (even if you want that type of pet), to respecting children's food allergies, even though you no longer have to account for the other spouse's dietary tastes. The same applies for vaping and smoking around a child with asthma. Even more than when you were a two-parent household, plan around any special needs your children have. An unscheduled trip to the hospital would not advance your long-term interests, because you placed your short-term interests over the children's best interests. Without specially indulging your children, make reasonable efforts to allow the children to maintain friendships and other social relationships. Similarly, while recognizing your children will almost certainly face extra and distracting stress, at least try to keep their grades from slipping. And repeating from earlier in the chapter, protect your children from learning about any of the tawdry details associated with your divorce, especially by not directly involving them in the litigation.

Despite that, sometimes one parent will want a child to testify to tell the judge his or her preferences. It is the judge's decision whether to disallow the child to be involved in the litigation, let the child openly testify, or speak to the child in the judge's chambers with only a court reporter and possibly allowing the parties' attorneys to be present.

If the child is 16 or 17 years old, and has voiced a preference for living with one of the parents, you then have to decide if it is worth a court battle, which is usually expensive to mount or defend, especially since the child will soon be considered an adult in many jurisdictions, once reaching 18 years old.[30] If you are the parent the child has chosen not to live with, you also have to consider that the child will be forced to go to court to testify against you. This puts the child in a very awkward position, which may have ramifications in your relationship with each other lasting well beyond the end of the divorce. You may consider foregoing this path of making a child choose which parent they want to live with, especially when the child is reticent to having to choose between you both.

Allow your children to love both parents, no matter how hurt or angry you are with your spouse. Ask yourself if you would be making the same parenting decision if you or your spouse were still together as a couple rather than letting yourself be guided by your anger or seek revenge.

Think of how you can make life better for the children while you are going through the divorce and afterward. Really listen to them rather than letting them feel like they are being dismissed, and if possible, set aside some real quality time, even if it is just a few minutes during the day. Remember, it is not the quantity but the quality of time you spend with your children that makes the difference.

CHAPTER 12

PARENTING PLANS—COMMONLY OVERLOOKED PROVISIONS

THE PARENTING PLAN IS THE DOCUMENT THAT DEFINES MANY ASPECTS OF how parents will raise their children. In Florida, this is a mandatory document for any divorce in which there are still minor children, and your jurisdiction will likely have a document with a similar purpose. Further, a number of jurisdictions, including Florida, require even private agreements reached about parenting decisions to be approved of by the trial court with findings that all of the plan's terms are in the best interests of the children.

THE BASIC PARENTING PLAN

There are some basic provisions that should be included in every parenting plan. The plan should identify both parents and include their mailing address, phone number, and email, as well as the full name of each child and date of birth. The jurisdiction that will be considered the children's home state should also be listed. Include that each parent has continuing responsibility to provide a current residential, mailing, and contact address as well as a contact phone number to the other parent and is required to notify the other parent within 24 hours of any changes. There should also be a requirement to notify the court in writing of any changes and within as many days as you and your lawyer decide is appropriate.

An important consideration is determining which parent has the ultimate decision-making authority or if this will be shared. In some jurisdictions, this is referred to as "legal custody." Major decisions that fall within this category include, but are not necessarily limited to, the children's education, healthcare, and other responsibilities unique to the family. A choice needs to be made regarding whether both parents will confer and jointly make all major decisions affecting their children's welfare, or if they can't agree then it must be decided which parent has the ultimate authority for each category. When there is an impasse under shared decision-making, often the only recourse is going to the judge for a ruling, but giving up decision-making authority on one or more issues does mean losing a significant amount of control over raising the children.

The parenting plan should include a provision that allows day-to-day decisions made by each parent while the children are with that parent. You don't want to forget to include that regardless of the allocation of ultimate decision-making authority, either parent may make emergency decisions affecting the health or safety of the children when residing with that parent. Any allowance for emergency decision-making should also include a directive to inform the other parent as soon as reasonably possible.

Extracurricular activities may play an important role in your children's lives, so these activities should be addressed. There are a number of options you can choose. For example, either parent may register the children and allow them to participate in the activity of the children's choice, or the parents must mutually agree to all extracurricular activities. You could also decide that one parent may unilaterally enroll a child in an activity only as long as it doesn't interfere with the other parent's time-sharing with the child. You need to decide who will transport the children to and from these extracurricular activities. There is the issue of who pays for, or the percentages paid by each parent, for the extracurricular activities, including the cost of uniforms, supplies, equipment, and travel.

Another important topic is the sharing of information from third parties. Unless otherwise prohibited by law, the parenting plan should provide for each parent to have access to school information and medical records pertaining to your children. You should both be permitted to independently consult with any professionals regarding your children. These professionals include daycare providers, healthcare providers, and other programs concerning the children's educational, emotional, and social progress. Both parents should have equal rights to inspect and receive governmental agency and law enforcement records concerning their children. This preferably includes being able to independently get all of this information without having to rely on the other parent. Make sure the parenting plan includes that both parents be listed as the children's emergency contacts.

More than just covering who provides for health insurance in the parenting plan, address noncovered items and the percentages each parent is required to pay. Uncovered insurance items could include dental, orthodontic, cosmetic, eye, hearing, and mental health treatment.

Scheduling is important and should be addressed. For school-aged children, pick a specific date that both parents obtain a copy of the school calendar for upcoming school years to plan for and reduce time-sharing/visitation conflicts caused by the school's schedule. This includes coordinating when school break periods differ between the schools your children attend. Cover school start dates, end dates, spring break, winter break, and any preplanned multiday closures.

A detailed yet accommodating time-sharing/visitation schedule often reduces misunderstandings and future litigation. In the event your jurisdiction does not require a parenting plan, be very specific in your time-sharing/visitation and legal custody sections of your agreement or relevant court order. Just calling for "liberal visitation" is inadequate and an invitation to further, frequent litigation during and after the divorce. The smartest way to approach time-sharing/visitation is to be as explicit as possible. You should have a weekday and weekend schedule that spells out the days of the week and times of the day that each parent has with the children. For overnights, the parenting plan should clearly reflect that. If different children need different schedules, specify those specific, individual schedules. Include what time of the day, afternoon, and/or evening the children will be exchanged between parents and where such exchanges will occur, be it at the parents' respective homes, at school, at a named midpoint restaurant, or even at a local police station.

Holidays and important personal days are often treated differently than the rest of the calendar. The most usual method we have seen is for the parties to list all the holidays that are important to them, and then alternate between them, so one parent gets time-sharing/visitation for one set of days on even years and another set on odd years. You should also choose a beginning and end time for the holiday visitation.

We have seen parenting plans where both parties share every Christmas, but where one party has included having Christmas evening and the following Christmas morning every year, which has left the other parent with the less favorable Christmas afternoon. A similar result occurs when one parent gets the first half of winter vacation every year—they get the entirety of Christmas while the other parent gets New Year's. A more equitable result would be to alternate the times each year.

The following is a nonexclusive list of holidays and special days you may want to consider including in your own parenting plan or agreement:
- Children's birthdays
- Christmas
- Columbus Day
- Diwali
- Easter
- Father's birthday
- Father's Day

- Fourth of July
- Halloween
- Hanukkah (Chanukah)
- Kwanzaa
- Labor Day
- Martin Luther King Day
- Memorial Day
- Mother's birthday
- Mother's Day
- New Year's Eve and Day
- Passover
- Presidents' Day
- Ramadan
- Rosh Hashanah
- Thanksgiving
- Veterans Day
- Yom Kippur

Part of considering how holidays and personal days affect the schedule is recognizing that these altered periods could give one parent a very large number of days in a row with the children. For example, some parents have whole alternating weeks with the children for the main time-sharing/visitation schedule, and when that directly follows Thanksgiving, one parent can have nearly two full weeks in a row. For parents who have one or two overnights during the week and alternating weekends, holiday schedules can wipe out most of those overnights for multiple contiguous weeks or months. If one parent will have three weekends in a row, the agreement could provide for the parent to forfeit the third weekend.[31]

The long summer break is another period during which parents are often allotted larger blocks of time with the children. For those parents who have less time during the school year but still want equal overall time with the children, summer provides the opportunity to make up that difference. Of course, summerlong activities like sleepaway camp could overlap and radically interfere with this time. Work with your lawyer to prevent such lopsided results from negatively affecting your ability to spend time with your children. Also understand that taking advantage of the other parent through scheduling is going to invite hostility and lead to litigation, even if the other side is likely to lose those hearings.

Another item to keep in mind is that many jurisdictions, including Florida, calculate child support based on the percentage of overnights during the year each parent has with the children. It is important to include the total amount of overnights for each parent in the parenting plan.

If transportation costs could be an issue, like situations where one parent lives a great distance from the other, that should be addressed. Who pays the cost of the flight and other public transportation? Who will accompany young children on the trip, and where will the children's exchange of parents take place? For peace of mind, the parenting plan should require the party taking the children to the airport to call the other party immediately upon departure to notify the other parent the children are arriving, and the party who meets the children must immediately notify the other party upon the children's arrival. Delineate the party responsible for notifying the other parent of flight and other travel delays.

What happens if you want to travel out of state or to a foreign country? The parenting plan can account for these travel considerations. Be aware that there is a difference between just giving notice or having to get permission from the other parent before traveling. Often, a parent will say "no" for no good reason, and there may not be sufficient time to get before a judge to overrule that parent's refusal.

If the agreement only requires notice, it should include giving the other parent written notice at least a certain amount of days before traveling out of state and a reasonably lengthier advance notice for traveling out of the country, unless there is an emergency. The parenting plan should also include a requirement for providing the other parent with a detailed itinerary for any long distance or duration trips, including locations and phone numbers where the children and parent can be reached. For parenting plans that allow international travel, require each parent to agree to providing whatever documentation is necessary for the other parent to take the children out of the country for the stated duration of the trip. Similarly, when allowing international travel, include in the parenting plan security measures to ensure the children's return.

If there is a concern that one parent may flee with the children to a jurisdiction outside the United States, have the parenting plan restrict travel to the United States and place secure control on how the children's passports will be held. The parenting plan can include enrolling the children in the Children's Passport Issuance Alert Program (CPIAP) of the United States Department of State.[32]

Education is another area to cover in the parenting plan. Florida, for example, requires that for purposes of school boundary determination and registration, one parent's address must be stated. That address can have far-reaching effects, especially if the parents live in different cities or even in different parts of a city. Attempting to move too far from that established address can become grounds in some jurisdictions to reevaluate the whole time-sharing/visitation schedule.

If the children will be attending private school, that should be included in the parenting plan, along with who is going to be paying the tuition and other costs, or the percentages each parent is responsible for. If the children are going to be homeschooled, it should be included in the parenting plan, along with what provisions are being made for homeschooling.

To ensure the parenting plan complies with various state and federal laws, such as the US Parental Kidnapping Prevention Act, the parenting plan must designate which parent the children will reside with for the majority of time. In jurisdictions that no longer follow designating one parent as having primary or majority physical custody and/or that allow for exactly 50/50 time-sharing/visitation, then include within the plan that this designation is included solely for the purpose of complying with the laws requiring such designation and otherwise has no force and effect on the parents or the children.

The parenting plan should specify the type of communication that will be used between the parents concerning their children. It may be in person; by telephone, letter, email, text message; and/or a communication program like TalkingParents or OurFamilyWizard. Better parenting plans further specify that the parents will not use the children as messengers to relay communication between the parents about matters covered by the parenting plan. Stick to using the specified means of communication, or if truly necessary, speak through your lawyer.

If there are any disputes that may arise over the terms of the parenting plan, it may provide that the parents shall seek to cooperatively attempt to resolve them by mediation, parenting coordinators, or parenting counselors before filing a court action. This can reduce litigation but also add time delays for matters destined to wind up before a judge.

Although these are basic provisions to consider for any parenting plan, we have seen situations that have arisen that were overlooked, creating what would have been unnecessary litigation.

AVOID COOKIE-CUTTER AGREEMENTS.

Too many agreements fail to include provisions not found in the most basic parenting plans, but which end up becoming critically contentious later on.

In jurisdictions that place extra emphasis on religious freedom, the trial court is unlikely to be able to simply pick a religion under which the children will be raised, or even one that should be avoided, unless a specific practice is found to be highly detrimental to the children. If you want to raise your children in a particular religion, include it in your agreement or parenting plan. However, we have still seen parents complain afterward. One parent complained about a parenting plan listing the child's religious upbringing, but that same parent had previously filed a proposed parenting plan insisting the child be raised in that same faith. Obviously, no post-divorce changes were made.

Other problems can arise with the holidays that are not usually foreseen in parenting plans or settlement agreements. For example, a Reform Jewish family may celebrate the holiday of Rosh Hashanah for only one day, so the agreement would probably alternate years for the holiday, while if they are Conservative or Orthodox Jews, they may celebrate that same holiday for two days. Therefore, an agreement should provide for alternating the first and second nights within the same year for the Conservative or Orthodox couple. Similar issues can arise for handling Ramadan, Diwali, Kwanzaa, and other holidays for which different groups with the same overarching religion or cultural celebrations have differing observation traditions.

Some parents, during and after a divorce, want no photographic reminders of the other parent anywhere in the home. This can lead to removing pictures and video from the children's rooms, phones, or computers. To prevent this from occurring, parenting plans have included instructions on what children are allowed to keep in the other parent's home and on the children's devices. If this is not spelled out in the parenting plan, then taking the other parent to court over destroyed pictures or video is far from an easy win despite the invasion of the children's privacy. What you may want can run headlong into the personal parenting style of the other parent and their general freedom in how to raise the children, unless already included in the parenting plan.

First right of refusal for unused time should be included in every parenting plan. This requires the parent who is unable to exercise time-sharing/visitation with the children to first offer that time to the other parent before having the child stay with a third party or be unaccompanied. The provisions normally result in the children spending much more time with the parents rather than being left in the care of third parties. Would you prefer to have extra time with your child when the other parent is unavailable due to work or wanting to take a weekend vacation? However, this provision needs to be thought through very carefully and personalized to your situation. A right of refusal that is only invoked when a whole overnight would occur without the parent being present goes untriggered should that parent begin working every afternoon through late evening. Conversely, while a 4-hour trigger will generally prevent that issue, it can have its own problems. One parent might like the idea of a first right of refusal after 4 hours so the children are not left in aftercare, until that same parent wants to go out for an evening and would prefer to use a babysitter rather than having the other parent know their plans, possibly losing a night of time-sharing if they stay out late in the evening. Additionally, your children wanting to spend most of one day playing at a friend's house would run afoul of this provision. Under a 4-hour period for first right of refusal, you would need to offer that time to the other parent or potentially be violating (in default of) your parenting plan.

Another item missing from many parenting plans is determining who can drop off and pick up the children from school, as well as who can stay with them. Will this include grandparents and other relatives, family friends, a person you are dating, or a new spouse? These considerations can become tricky, especially if either parent is starting a new relationship. Similarly, you need to plan for how this would interact with a first right of refusal provision when you are not going to be physically present at the start of such time-sharing/visitation periods.

You will want to include provisions dealing with a parent who is late in dropping off or picking up the children so that, unless advance notice is given, if they are more than a certain amount of minutes late then they lose that visitation. Spell out the consequences for repeated violations if you feel that would fit your situation.

When the children become old enough to drive, there is the issue of vehicle insurance. These premiums can add a substantial expense that many parents with younger children do not consider when establishing a parenting plan. Similarly, will there be a provision as to who pays for the first or any replacement vehicles?

We have heard parents complain that they send clothing and other personal items with the children when they have overnights with the other parent, but these items never seem to be returned. The parenting plan should address this eventuality by requiring that the children have sufficient clothing packed when there is a time-sharing/visitation exchange, and all of the same items that accompanied the children be returned when the children come back, or may require each parent to have a full wardrobe for the children at their house.

Another issue that is hurtful to parents but is often omitted from parenting plans is requiring that only the biological parents can be called Mom or Dad, or other similar names typically used to refer to the parents. Often, when one parent remarries or is in a serious relationship, there is a tendency to encourage children to call the new person some variation of Mom or Dad. This can be part of a deliberate attempt to hurt the other parent or an innocent progression of a relationship between the children and that person. However, including this provision in the parenting plan will go a long way toward eliminating concerns over the issue.

ESTABLISH LIMITATIONS ON DEVICES/INTERNET/ SOCIAL MEDIA/AI USE BY CHILDREN

You and your spouse should decide at what age your children can have a phone. General usage of electronic devices and internet access, including considerations for parental filters and GPS tracking, can be included. When coming to this decision, do you have concerns that your spouse may track you through your child's phone's GPS during your time-sharing/visitation? Will there be an issue if the GPS is disabled? Who will pay for the cost of the phone, including the usage fees and app-related purchases?

Will the children have tablets and/or other computers, and if so, who is responsible to pay for, upgrade, and/or replace them? Additionally, address who pays for damaged, lost, or stolen devices and the timeframe for replacing these items.

DETERMINE THE DISTANCE A PARENT CAN MOVE WITHOUT COURT APPROVAL

Will you be limiting moving to a particular city, county or counties, or by mileage? Moving beyond that zone is called relocation. The basic idea of these provisions is to limit disruption to the children's lives that would be caused by spending too much travel time commuting between parents' homes, to school, and the children's other common travel destinations. Therefore, parents are not free to move wherever they want with the children. Move too far without demonstrating to the court that the move is in the best interests of the children (with you benefiting as a side effect), and the court can order that your intended, or already in-progress, move will happen without the children. They will remain with the other parent, and you could lose a substantial portion of your time-sharing/visitation, along with an accompanying recalculation of child support. As soon as an initial home address is established for the children, and even before a parenting plan is otherwise in effect, the parents can be subject to the local jurisdiction's relocation rules.

Where the local jurisdiction allows, we have seen parenting plans revise the rule on distance to alternatively limit the ability to move based on either distance or a named geographic area such as a set number of miles, or a county, or tri-county area. In Florida, for example, distances are based upon a linear distance of "as the crow flies" rather than based on roads and driving distances, and one party can move from their home within 50 miles as the crow flies without filing a petition for relocation.[33] Someone who uses the statutory measurement can actually move for many more driving miles if the route is not in a straight line (for example, routes with highways with long gaps between off-ramps, detours, or winding roads). Remember, the more nonlinear distance and the more obstructions in the route, the more time the children will be forced to spend traveling. Then again, there are parents who purposefully move right next to the edge of the border as a strategy to facilitate formal relocation when the true, intended final home is just a few more miles down the road, or out of spite.

Because of this important distinction, if there is the possibility of one party moving within the statutory limits or seeking to relocate, if you are in a jurisdiction that calculates distance in a single, straight line, then you may want your parenting plan to instead limit based on driving distance as calculated by the shortest toll-free or toll road travel through a specific mapping program.

CHILDREN'S ACCOUNTS

Some parents establish 529 college savings accounts for their children. A 529 account is a state-sponsored investment plan that enables you to save money for your children and pay for educational expenses such as tuition, books, and school supplies. These plans allow tax-free withdrawals for these expenses, and plan holders may also be eligible for additional state or federal tax benefits. There are also prepaid college accounts. Many parents and/or relatives will establish regular savings, checking, and/or investment accounts in the name of one or more children and/or with one or both parents listed on the account. Cover all of these accounts in the parenting plan to prevent the risk of the other parent liquidating the accounts, which we have seen happen far too often. Any other significant, costly, or hard-to-replace personal possessions for the children can also be listed, with grounds limiting the terms under which these possessions could be sold by a parent.

HIGHER EDUCATION

Some states, like Florida, do not require parents to pay for children's postsecondary education, like college and postgraduate studies, so if somebody is going to be required to pay, then it must be negotiated for in the parenting plan. Other states allow courts to directly order payment for higher education. You need to check if payment for children's later education is included in your jurisdiction.

USE OF ALCOHOL AND OTHER DRUGS

If you or your spouse have a drug or alcohol problem, the parenting plan should include some level of random hair/urine testing for a period of time so your children are protected. We have seen agreements that do not permit the parent with a known alcohol or drug problem to drive a motor vehicle or boat with their children inside the vehicle during their time-sharing. Other parenting plans have included blanket restrictions on usage of legal substances during and/or immediately before any time-sharing/visitation with the children, even when a parent's prior history has never risen to the level of an actual problem. Such restrictions prevent problems from impacting the children. Of course, that restriction is double-edged, in that it prevents a parent from also reasonably enjoying, unwinding, or celebrating a special event with a drink, whether at home, at a restaurant, at a networking function, or on a date. When your attorney drafts the agreement, it is important to think through all the possible consequences so you can particularize it to fit your situation.

OTHER CONSIDERATIONS

Other items that can be included in a parenting plan concern when a parent can introduce the children to a significant other (for example, they must have been dating for at least six months); giving the spouse the opportunity to meet the significant other before the children; not having the significant other sleep over when the children are present unless engaged; no piercings or tattoos without both parents' approval; no guns around the children and no taking children to gun ranges without both parents' approval; and no R-rated movies until the children are a certain age.

TEMPORARY PARENTING PLANS

There is the permanent parenting plan issued at the end of your divorce, which will carry you through your and your children's post-divorce life, and there can also be temporary parenting plans that put all parties on notice as to their parental responsibilities during the divorce. Remember, you cannot enforce an agreement or order that does not yet exist. Having a temporary parenting plan solves that problem. Every issue discussed in this chapter can be covered in a temporary parenting plan. Most importantly, this will enable you to secure make-up time for being denied access to your children and can potentially reduce the number of times you need to try to secure a hearing (which could be weeks or months out) to get a court ruling each time there is a disagreement over the children.

In summary, you need to think about your own situation and what is important to you, your spouse, and your children. Protect yourself from future heartache and litigation costs by including those issues in your parenting plan or agreement.

CHILDREN'S THERAPISTS, ATTORNEYS AD LITEM, GUARDIANS AD LITEM, AND SOCIAL INVESTIGATIONS

You should expect changes in your children's physical and emotional health when you are contemplating divorce and during the divorce proceedings with your spouse. It is not unusual for children to be depressed or to act out. Your children may have some physical complaints, like headaches or stomachaches. Some children regress, such as a toddler who is no longer potty-trained, or a student whose grades take a downward spiral. Other children may have nightmares, have trouble sleeping, or sleep too much. Just as you may consider counseling for yourself, your children may also benefit from counseling.

THERAPISTS

There are therapists who specialize in helping children through their parents' divorce. However, you should take special care in your selection, as not all therapists are the same, and you should look for a therapist who will interact in a way that allows your children to feel comfortable opening up and speaking honestly. Talk with your divorce attorney about recommendations; they most likely have experience with different therapists and feedback from former clients. Friends whose children went through therapy are another source. You can also look at online reviews. In some contentious divorces, each side may pick a therapist, and if they are unable to work it out, the judge will make the ultimate decision.

Therapists are sometimes ordered for family reunification, when one spouse is estranged from the child. We have seen instances where one spouse will attempt to fire the therapist if they feel the sessions are not going favorably for them. Court intervention may be needed to preclude this from happening, but the therapist could decide not to continue with the reunification sessions as a result of this conflict.

Beware of therapists who are hired because they have a professional relationship with an attorney for one of the parties and have consistently testified in favor of their client. They may have an unconscious or conscious bias. Have your counsel find out how often that therapist is selected by opposing counsel, as this may enter into whether you will agree to that therapist. Talk to your attorney for their opinion regarding whether this will be a problem for your children and your case.

In Florida, the therapist has a psychotherapist-patient privilege with the children.[34] This means the child-patient has a privilege to refuse to disclose, and to prevent anyone else from disclosing, confidential communications or records made for the purpose of treatment of the child's mental or emotional condition.[35] This issue can sometimes be resolved with the appointment of an attorney ad litem, a court-appointed lawyer who represents a child during the course of a legal action, such as a divorce.[36]

ATTORNEY AD LITEM

An attorney representing a child as the child's attorney ad litem is expected to represent the child in the same manner as if they were representing an adult client. The attorney is expected to advocate on behalf of the child, and most importantly, to advocate for the expressed wishes of the child. In order to perform these duties, the attorney must be able to effectively communicate with the child so the child can understand the options available and make an informed decision. There is also a duty of confidentiality owed to the child client that goes along with representation.

We have most often seen the appointment of an attorney ad litem where a parent wants to see the child's therapist's records relating to their child or have the child's therapist testify in custody or time-sharing litigation. Since there is a confidentiality attached to this information, the child's attorney ad litem is in the position to speak for the child's wishes regarding this matter. Some children don't want their parents to learn what was said about them in the sessions the child has had with the therapist, while others are fine with their records being released.

Attorneys ad litem also represent the wishes of their child clients in other issues that may arise during the divorce proceedings. For example, they may be requested to speak to the social investigator about a particular problem the child is too frightened or anxious to raise on their own because of parental threats or pressures. The attorney ad litem attends hearings related to issues that arise and advocates for their client's wishes.

GUARDIAN AD LITEM

The guardian ad litem's role is distinctively different than that of the attorney ad litem. While the attorney ad litem's role is to advocate for the child's expressed wishes, the guardian ad litem's role is to act on behalf of the "best interests of the child." In some states, an attorney who is permitted to act as both a guardian ad litem and the child's attorney is sometimes referred to as a "hybrid attorney."[37] However, this can cause an ethical and legal conflict when the child's expressed wishes and their best interests are in conflict. That is why in Florida, the child's guardian ad litem and attorney ad litem cannot be the same person.[38]

For example, during the divorce proceedings, the children may be swayed by the behavior of one parent, who buys them expensive gifts and relaxes rules both parents had previously enforced during their intact marriage. The children express their desire to spend more time-sharing/ visitation with the newly indulgent parent, but the guardian ad litem, who is aware of how that parent is manipulating the children, would not advance what the children presently want but instead what is in their best interests.[39]

In Florida, the guardian ad litem is given broad investigatory powers, to interview the child and witnesses, or any other person having information concerning the child's welfare. They may petition the court to obtain records from hospitals, medical doctors, dentists, psychologists, and psychiatrists, and request the court to order expert examinations of the child, the child's parents, or other interested parties in the action, by any of these same medical professionals.[40] Some attorneys will try to have the guardian ad litem speak to their client first, so that spouse will be able to present their side of the story first.

In Florida, the guardian ad litem is required to file with the court, and on all parties, a written report which may include recommendations and a statement of the wishes of the child. However, because the report usually contains information that can be objected to as "hearsay,"[41] we often see the guardian ad litem have the parties and their attorneys sign an agreement that will waive any hearsay objection that may appear in the report and during the testimony of the guardian ad litem at a deposition or in court. A report may be structured around your jurisdiction's best interest factors, which were explained in Chapter 11.

Because of the broad powers of the guardian ad litem to investigate and speak to many different witnesses, there are judges who rely upon their recommendations in making the decision regarding custody/ time-sharing/visitation and whether one parent will have the ultimate authority to decide in one or more areas of the child's life regarding education, medical decisions, and extracurricular activities. It is therefore most important to be on your best behavior and to cooperate with the guardian ad litem.

SOCIAL INVESTIGATIONS

In Florida, in any action where time-sharing, parental responsibility, ultimate decision-making, or a parenting plan for the children is in controversy, the court, on its own or on the motion of any party, may order a social investigation and study concerning all the pertinent details relating to the children and each parent for that case.[42] One major difference in Florida between the reports of a guardian ad litem and a social investigator is that by statute, the court may consider the information contained in the social investigator's study in making a decision on the parenting plan, as the technical rules of evidence do not exclude the study from consideration by the court.[43] Usually, in Florida, the social investigation is conducted by a psychologist, a clinical social worker, a marriage and family therapist, or a licensed mental health counselor.[44]

The parents may be given psychological and personality tests, as well as tests that help to determine substance abuse tendencies and screening if those issues are germane to the case. The social investigator usually includes home visits to observe the parents' interactions with the children in their home, and the social investigator may speak to a variety of people who have some knowledge about the children or their parents. This group can include school personnel; the children's medical doctors, dentists, and therapists; the parents' relatives; and persons whom the parents have requested be included in the interviews.

Once the investigation and study are concluded, a report is provided to the court and the parties. In Florida, the report is required to contain recommendations, including a written statement of facts found in the social investigation upon which the recommendations are based. Judges often rely on this report and the testimony of the social investigator in making a decision regarding the parenting plan.

Similar to meeting with a guardian ad litem, some attorneys attempt to schedule their client's appointment with the social investigator first, so the investigator interviews their client before the other parent, who may be left in the position of defending themselves instead of being on the offensive. It is advisable to be honest and forthright with the investigator, to be on time for all appointments, and to cooperate fully to enhance your possibility of having a favorable determination.

THE IMPORTANCE OF KNOWING YOUR FINANCES

It's your divorce—you carry the ultimate burden for your outcome!

One of the most important aspects of many divorces concerns finances. Your attorney will need financial documents for issues concerning alimony, child support, and equitable distribution (distribution of assets and liabilities). Financial documents may also be crucial to determining what the judge will consider to be marital or nonmarital assets and liabilities. As explained earlier in Chapter 9, "discovery" is the pretrial phase of a lawsuit during which you seek to learn more about your spouse's case by gathering information through four major ways: depositions, interrogatories, requests for production, and requests for admission.

As discussed in Chapter 4, it is best if you can gather the documents before filing for divorce, as they have a tendency to disappear after one spouse files for divorce. There is a danger if your attorney is unable to get all the necessary documentation because you may then be unable to fully present your case, allowing your spouse to get away with hiding and keeping assets.

Remember this important phrase when it comes to the discovery phase of the divorce litigation: "If you don't ask, you don't get!"

There are a number of different financial documents you can use as a starting point for your own financial discovery:

- Each spouse's financial affidavit.
- All complete federal and state personal tax returns, gift tax returns, and foreign tax returns for the past 3 years, with all attachments, including your W-2s, 1099s, and K-1s for those years, and all accompanying schedules and worksheets.
- Proof of income with pay stubs or evidence of income for the past 6 months.
- A statement identifying the amount and all sources of income received for the past six months, if not indicated by a pay stub.
- All loan applications, financial statements, credit reports, or any other form of financial disclosure, financial aid forms, or any document used for the purpose of obtaining credit or loans in the prior 24 months.
- All deeds showing any ownership interest in property during the prior 3 years.
- Promissory notes or leases showing money owed in the last 24 months.
- Any trusts or guardianships from which you received a payment in the last 3 years or own an interest.
- All statements from checking accounts, savings accounts, money market funds, and certificates of deposit (regardless of whether or not the accounts have been closed) for which you are named as an account holder, including any joint accounts during the last 12 months.
- Copies of canceled checks and registers, whether written or electronically maintained, within the last 12 months.
- All brokerage statements for which your name appears as an account holder for the past 12 months.

- All statements for any profit sharing, retirement, deferred compensation, or pension plan (like an IRA, 401(k), 403(b), SEP, Keogh, or other similar accounts) for the past 12 months as well as the most recent statement from each account.
- All statements for the past 12 months for any virtual currency transaction in which you or your spouse participated, as well as a listing of all current holdings of virtual currencies (like Bitcoin, Ethereum, NFTs, or any other digital currency).
- Declaration page, the last periodic statement, statements for the past 12 months, and the certificate for all life insurance policies insuring your life or your spouse's life, as well as health and dental insurance cards covering you, your spouse, and/or your dependent children.
- Corporate, partnership, and trust tax returns for the last 3 years, if you have an ownership or interest in a corporation, partnership, or trust, along with profit and loss statements.
- All written agreements entered into at any time between the parties either prior to or during their marriage.
- All documents supporting a claim that an asset is nonmarital, for enhancement or appreciation of nonmarital property or for an unequal division of marital property.
- Any court order directing a party to pay or receive spousal or child support.[45]

Often, a forensic accountant,[46] who is usually a certified public accountant (CPA), is retained by your lawyer on your behalf to go through all of the financial documents. The CPA is an important component in your divorce arsenal, especially when there are substantial assets, complex financial situations, or a spouse you suspect is lying about their finances, and may be hiding money. The judge will be looking for facts about the parties' marital and nonmarital assets and liabilities, and a CPA can be invaluable in providing this information. The CPA is often used to find hidden assets, provide a lifestyle analysis of the parties during their marriage, and determine what the financial needs of their client will be after the divorce, as well as determine the other spouse's ability to pay. They can also spot inconsistencies in the financial documents that will go toward credibility. For example, credit reports or financial statements that are filled out when seeking a loan or to make a substantial purchase can be compared with the spouse's financial affidavit to find inconsistencies. Sometimes the CPA or an expert business evaluator will be used to provide valuations for a business that either or both parties may have some interest in.

The CPA may uncover a potential area of hidden assets. Be sure to have your lawyer follow up if your spouse fails to provide the full discovery you have requested and any additional discovery the CPA deems important to your case. We have had numerous potential clients complain about how their attorneys failed to pursue the financial trail of critical assets, causing these people to suffer because of the inability to prove the other spouse's true income and assets. Unfortunately, these clients rarely get relief on appeal because of their attorney's laxity in pursuing discovery. While other aspects of a divorce might be reversible, when there is a simple lack of proper evidence before the trial court, it is often unfixable on appeal.

There are remedies that can be implemented when a spouse fails to produce requested documents. For example, if there are missing bank checks, credit card or brokerage account statements, subpoenas can be issued to those institutions to produce the requested items. If the CPA finds secret accounts, the bank will normally have to honor the subpoena.

Motions can also be filed against your spouse. In Florida, your lawyer can file a motion to compel if your spouse has not provided you with the requested discovery, and if court orders directing the production of this evidence still do not provide results, your lawyer can file a motion seeking to hold your spouse in contempt. Being found in contempt can be quite painful, as the court may:

- Enter an order requiring your spouse to pay your legal fees for the time spent by your lawyer in having to file the motion and attend a hearing.
- Enter an order fining your spouse for every day there is a delay in providing the discovery.
- Impute that your spouse has the ability to pay concerning the issue at hand, such as the ability to pay the alimony or child support the judge awards.
- Send your spouse to jail until the requested discovery is provided.
- Any combination of these remedies.[47]

When trying to find out your spouse's true income, there are a number of different types of income to consider:

1. Salary or wages.
2. Bonuses, commissions, allowances, overtime, tips, and other similar payments.
3. Business income from sources such as self-employment, partnership, close corporations, and independent contracts. "Business income" means gross receipts minus ordinary and necessary expenses required to produce income.
4. Disability benefits.
5. All workers' compensation benefits and settlements.
6. Reemployment assistance or unemployment compensation.
7. Pension, retirement, or annuity payments.
8. Social security benefits.
9. Spousal support received from a previous marriage or court ordered in the marriage before the court.
10. Interest and dividends.
11. Rental income, which is gross receipts minus ordinary and necessary expenses required to produce the income.
12. Income from royalties, trusts, or estates.

13. Reimbursed expenses or in kind payments to the extent that they reduce living expenses. (In kind payments are the use of goods or services rather than using money).[48]

14. Gains derived from dealings in property, unless the gain is nonrecurring.[49]

Sometimes we have frustrated clients who complain they provided their divorce lawyer with documents that were never presented at trial. If you believe a particular document or set of documents is important to your case, you should speak to your attorney prior to the trial so there is an understanding of whether or not they will be used at trial, and if not, the reasons why your attorney does not want to or cannot enter them into evidence. There may be problems with authenticating the document, or a hearsay problem, or another legal basis that prevents the lawyer from introducing the document at trial.

It is vitally important that you promptly, truthfully, and accurately respond to all discovery requests directed to you in the divorce litigation. Don't just rely on your attorney to fill out your financial affidavit, respond to interrogatories, or attempt to get the financial documents that have been requested from you. Help your lawyer in this process; after all, it is ultimately your case! You must swear to the truthfulness of the answers to the interrogatories and the numbers listed on your financial affidavit. You want this to be as accurate as possible. The more information you are able to provide to back up your claims, the better chance you have of prevailing on that issue. To the extent that the discovery requested might be overly broad, unreasonably intrusive, or an outright fishing expedition being done just to see what might turn up, have your lawyer timely respond with an appropriate objection since you cannot sit on the discovery request.

At the start of your divorce, and certainly no later than when dealing with the first batch of discovery, is the time to consult with your financial advisor, broker, insurance agent, realtor, accountant, and anybody else whose personal knowledge is going to affect your finances during and after the divorce. Too often, these professionals are consulted on the eve of trial, when it's too late for them to give appropriate, divorce-altering advice and prepare potential evidence for your case. Worse, some people do not even speak with these professionals until after the marital settlement agreement is signed or the final judgment has been entered granting the divorce, only to then learn just how badly damaged their whole post-divorce life is going to be due to this self-inflicted ignorance.

One last piece of advice. If your spouse already has a major relationship with these advisors or agents, you should really look into getting your own so that there will be no conflict of interest and no back-channel sharing of your sensitive information. There is no need to give away your divorce strategy in advance because your shared advisor might happen to have a closer relationship with your spouse than with you.

COMMON MISTAKES MADE IN PREPARING FINANCIAL AFFIDAVITS

THE FAMILY LAW FINANCIAL AFFIDAVIT IS ONE OF THE MOST CRITICAL documents in your divorce case. Divorces are won and lost based on the content of the financial affidavit. This detailed document informs the court of your income, expenses, including expenses for your children, as well as assets and liabilities. The following sample,[50] which you should take the time to review, shows a nonexclusive list of items to cover in your affidavit and to verify the other spouse is including in their affidavit:

SECTION I. INCOME
PRESENT MONTHLY GROSS INCOME:

1. _____ Gross salary or wages
2. _____ Bonuses, commissions, allowances, overtime, tips, and similar payments
3. _____ Business income from sources such as self-employment, partnerships, close corporations, and/or independent contracts (Gross receipts minus ordinary and necessary expenses required to produce income.) (Attach sheet itemizing such income and expenses.)
4. _____ Disability benefits/SSI
5. _____ Workers' compensation
6. _____ Reemployment assistance

7. _____ Pension, retirement, or annuity payments

8. _____ Social Security benefits

9. _____ Alimony actually received (Add 9a and 9b)

     9a. From this case: _____

     9b. From other case(s): _____

10. _____ Interest and dividends

11. _____ Rental income (gross receipts minus ordinary and necessary expenses required to produce income) (Attach sheet itemizing such income and expenses for each property.)

12. _____ Income from royalties, trusts, or estates

13. _____ Reimbursed expenses and in-kind payments to the extent that they reduce personal living expenses (Attach sheet itemizing such income and expenses.)

14. _____ Gains derived from dealing in property (not including nonrecurring gains)

   _____ Any other income of a recurring nature (identify source):

15. _____

16. _____

17. $_____ **TOTAL PRESENT MONTHLY GROSS INCOME** (Add lines 1 through 16.)

PRESENT MONTHLY DEDUCTIONS:

18. _____ Federal, state, and local income tax (corrected for filing status and allowable dependents and income tax liabilities)

     18a. Filing Status _____

     18b. Number of dependents claimed _____

19. _____ FICA or self-employment taxes

20. _____ Medicare payments

21. _____ Mandatory union dues

22. _____ Mandatory retirement payments

23. _____ Health insurance payments for you only (including medical, dental, and vision), excluding portion paid for any third party or minor children of this relationship

24. _____ Court-ordered child support actually paid for children from another relationship

25. _____ Court-ordered alimony actually paid
(Add 25a and 25b)
25a. From this case: _____
25b. From other case(s): _____

26. $_____ **TOTAL DEDUCTIONS ALLOWABLE UNDER SECTION 61.30, FLORIDA STATUTES** (Add lines 18 through 25.)

27. $_____ **PRESENT NET MONTHLY INCOME** (Subtract line 26 from line 17.)

SECTION II. AVERAGE MONTHLY EXPENSES

PRIMARY HOUSEHOLD:

List the number of additional households for which you incur expenses (If more than one household, please identify the household for which the listed expenses are incurred and attach a separate sheet listing expenses for each additional household.)

1. _____ Mortgage or rent payments

2. _____ Property taxes (if not included in mortgage)

3. _____ Insurance on residence (if not included in mortgage)

4. _____ Condominium maintenance fees and homeowner's association fees

5. _____ Electricity

6. _____ Water, garbage, and sewer

7. _____ Telephone

8. _____ Fuel oil or natural gas

9. _____ Repairs and maintenance

10. _____ Lawn care

11. _____ Pool maintenance

12. _______ Pest control
13. _______ Misc. household
14. _______ Food and home supplies
15. _______ Meals outside home
16. _______ Cable t.v./internet
17. _______ Subscription streaming services
18. _______ Alarm service contract
19. _______ Service contracts on appliances
20. _______ Housekeeping service
21. _______ Communication technology/ remote working subscriptions

Other:

22. ______________________________________
23. ______________________________________
24. ______________________________________
25. ______________________________________
26. ______________________________________
27. $_____ **Subtotal** (Add lines 1 through 26.)

AUTOMOBILES:

List the number of automobiles for which you incur expenses: _______.

28. _______ Gasoline and oil
29. _______ Electric car charging (outside of the home)
30. _______ Repairs
31. _______ Auto tags
32. _______ Insurance
33. _______ Payments (lease or financing)
34. _______ Rental
35. _______ Alternative transportation (bus, rail, carpool, taxi, ridesharing, etc.)
36. _______ Tolls and parking
37. _______ Automobile subscriptions and roadside services

38. _____ Other: _____

39. $_____ **SUBTOTAL** (Add lines 28 through 38)

MONTHLY EXPENSES FOR MINOR OR DEPENDENT CHILDREN COMMON TO BOTH PARTIES:

40. _____ Childcare

41. _____ School tuition

42. _____ School supplies, books, and fees

43. _____ Extracurricular activities

44. _____ School uniforms

45. _____ Lunch money

46. _____ Private lessons or tutoring

47. _____ Allowances

48. _____ Clothing

49. _____ Entertainment (movies, parties, video games, etc.)

50. _____ Health insurance (including dental and vision)

51. _____ Medical, dental, prescriptions (nonreimbursed only)

52. _____ Psychiatric/psychological/counselor

53. _____ Orthodontic

54. _____ Grooming

55. _____ Nonprescription medications, supplements, and vitamins

56. _____ Cosmetics, toiletries, and sundries

57. _____ Gifts from child(ren) to others (other children, relatives, teachers, etc.)

58. _____ Camp or summer activities

59. _____ Clubs (Boy/Girl Scouts, etc.)

60. _____ Cost required to exercise time-sharing (supervised visitation, travel and lodging expenses, etc.)

61. _____ Religious training

62. _____ Remote learning

63. _____ Subscription service (if not listed on line 17 above)

64. _____ Other
65. $_____ **SUBTOTAL** (Add lines 40 through 64.)

MONTHLY EXPENSES FOR MINOR OR DEPENDENT CHILD(REN) FROM ANOTHER RELATIONSHIP

(other than court-ordered child support)

66. _____
67. _____
68. _____
69. _____
70. $_____ **SUBTOTAL** (Add lines 66 through 69.)

MONTHLY INSURANCE:

71. _____ Health insurance
    (if not listed on lines 23 of deductions or 50 of expenses)
72. _____ Life insurance
73. _____ Dental insurance
    (if not listed on lines 23 of deductions or 50 of expenses)
74. _____ Vision insurance
    (if not listed on lines 23 of deductions or 50 of expenses)
75. _____ Long term care insurance
76. _____ Disability insurance
Other:
77. _____
78. _____
79. $_____ **SUBTOTAL** (Add lines 71 through 78)

OTHER MONTHLY EXPENSES NOT LISTED ABOVE:

80. _____ Dry cleaning and laundry
81. _____ Clothing
82. _____ Medical, dental, and prescription
    (unreimbursed only)

83. _____ Psychiatric, psychological, or counselor (unreimbursed only)

84. _____ Nonprescription medications, cosmetics, toiletries, and sundries

85. _____ Grooming

86. _____ Gifts

87. _____ Pet care

88. _____ Club dues and membership

89. _____ Sports and hobbies

90. _____ Entertainment

91. _____ Periodicals/books/other subscription service

92. _____ Charitable donations

93. _____ Gambling and lottery

94. _____ Tobacco, alcohol, and vaping

95. _____ Attorney fees and court costs

        95a. _____ Related to this case

        95b._____ Other

96. _____ Professional training fees (unreimbursed only)

97. _____ Vacations

98. _____ Religious organizations

99. _____ Bank charges/credit card fees

100. _____ Education expenses (unreimbursed only)

101. _____ Other: (include any regular and recurring expenses not otherwise mentioned in the items listed above)_____

_____

102. _____

103. _____

104. _____

105. $_____ **SUBTOTAL** (Add lines 80 through 104.)

MONTHLY PAYMENTS TO CREDITORS:

List only when payments are currently made by you on outstanding balances and not listed elsewhere on this affidavit. For student loans listed below, list **each** student loan together with its date of origination. List only last 4 digits of account numbers.

MONTHLY PAYMENT AND NAME OF CREDITOR(S):

106. _____

107. _____

108. _____

109. _____

110. _____

111. _____

112. _____

113. _____

114. _____

115. _____

116. _____

117. _____

118. _____

119. $_____ **SUBTOTAL** (Add lines 106 through 118.)

120. $_____ **TOTAL MONTHLY EXPENSES:** (Add lines 27, 39, 65, 70, 79, 105, and 119 of Section II, Expenses.)

SUMMARY

121. $_____ **TOTAL PRESENT MONTHLY NET INCOME** (from line 27 of SECTION I. INCOME)

122. $_____ **TOTAL MONTHLY EXPENSES** (from line 120 above)

123. $_____ **SURPLUS** (If line 121 is more than line 122, subtract line 122 from line 121. This is the amount of your surplus. Enter that amount here.)

124. $ (____) **(DEFICIT)** (If line 122 is more than line 121, subtract line 121 from line 122. This is the amount of your deficit. Enter that amount here.)

SECTION III. ASSETS AND LIABILITIES

Requesting to be Awarded	A ASSETS: DESCRIPTION OF ITEM(S) List Only Last Four Digits of Account Numbers. *Check the box on the left in column A next to any asset(s) which you are requesting be awarded to you.*	Title Owner	B MARITAL ASSETS – Current Fair Market Value	C NONMARITAL ASSETS – Current Fair Market Value PETITIONER	RESPONDENT
	Cash (on hand)		$		
	Cash (in banks and credit unions, including checking, savings and money market accounts, certificates of deposit, and in safe deposit boxes)				
	Cash (in digital wallets, including but not limited to Venmo, Apple Wallet, and PayPal)				
	Virtual currency and cryptocurrency (attach a schedule that shows number of units held of virtual currency or cryptocurrency and unit value at time of preparation of this form)				
	Non-Fungible Tokens (NFT) and the like				
	Stocks/Bonds, investment/brokerage accounts				
	Notes (money owed to you in writing)				
	Money owed to you (not evidenced by a note)				
	Real estate: (Home)				
	Real estate (Other)				

	Business interests (also indicate % of ownership interest next to each entity listed)			
	Automobiles			
	Boats			
	Other vehicles			
	Retirement plans (Profit Sharing, Pension, IRA, 401(k)s, etc.)			
	Furniture & furnishings in home			
	Furniture & furnishings elsewhere			
	Collectibles and commodities (including but not limited to cards, precious metals, coins, stamps, and art)			
	Jewelry			
	Life insurance (cash surrender value)			
	Sporting, hobby, and entertainment (T.V., stereo, etc.) equipment			
	Tools			
	Firearms and ammunition			
	Judgments (owed to you)			

	Patents, trademarks, copyrights				
	Other assets:				
Total Fair Market Value of Marital Assets (add column B)			$		
Total Fair Market Value of Nonmarital Assets (add column C)			$		

A LIABILITIES: DESCRIPTION OF ITEM(S) List Only Last Four Digits of Account Numbers. *Check the box on the left of column A next to any debt(s) for which you believe you should be responsible.*				**B** MARITAL LIABILITIES— Current Amount Owed	**C** NONMARITAL LIABILITIES— Current Amount Owed	
					PETITIONER	**RESPONDENT**
Requesting to be Responsible for		**Debtor/ Obligor/ Title Holder**	**Creditor**			
	Mortgages on real estate			$		
	Charge/credit card accounts					
	Student loans (list each loan individually)					

	Medical liabilities					
	Auto loans					
	Bank/Credit Union loans					
	Tax liabilities					
	Notes (money you owe in writing)					
	Money you owe (not evidenced by a note)					
	Judgments (against you)					
	Other liabilities:					
Total Amount Owed on Marital Liabilities (add column B)			$			
Total Amount Owed on Nonmarital Liabilities (add column C)			$			

C. NET WORTH (EXCLUDING CONTINGENT ASSETS AND LIABILITIES)

$_____ TOTAL ASSETS

(enter total of Column B in Asset Table; Section A)

$_____ TOTAL LIABILITIES

(enter total of Column B in Liabilities Table; Section B)

$_____ TOTAL NET WORTH (Total Assets minus Total Liabilities)

(excluding contingent assets and liabilities)

D. CONTINGENT ASSETS AND LIABILITIES

INSTRUCTIONS:

If you have any **POSSIBLE assets** (possible lawsuits, income potential, accrued vacation or sick leave, bonus, inheritance, etc.) or **POSSIBLE liabilities** (possible lawsuits, future unpaid taxes, contingent tax liabilities, debts assumed by another), you must list them here.

A CONTINGENT ASSETS *Check the box on the left in column A next to any contingent asset(s) which you are requesting be awarded to you.*			B MARITAL CONTINGENT ASSETS – Possible Value	C NONMARITAL CONTINGENT ASSETS – Possible Value	
				PETITIONER	RESPONDENT
Requesting to be Awarded		Title Owner	$		
	Stock Options				
	Other				
Total Possible Value of Marital Contingent Assets (add column B)			$		
Total Possible Value of Nonmarital Contingent Assets (add column C)			$		

A CONTINGENT LIABILITIES *Check the box in column A next to any contingent debt(s) for which you believe you should be responsible.*				B MARITAL CONTINGENT LIABILITIES – Possible Amount Owed	C NONMARITAL CONTINGENT LIABILITIES– Possible Amount Owed	
					PETITIONER	RESPONDENT
Requesting to be Responsible For		Debtor/ Obligor/ Title Holder	Creditor	$	$	$
	Attorney Fees					
Total Possible Amount Owed on Contingent Liabilities				$	$	$

Florida Family Law Rules of Procedure Form 12.902(c), Family Law Financial Affidavit (Long Form) (06/25)

Be extremely careful in completing your financial affidavit because affidavits are sworn statements to the court, meaning everything contained in the affidavit is the absolute truth as you understood it at the time you prepared the document. Accuracy is key. Your spouse's attorney will look for any inconsistencies they can find and will attempt to poke holes in the document. It is important to substantiate your numbers with documents like credit card statements, bank records, receipts, and appraisals.

Avoid obviously inflated or deflated numbers as a means to try to manipulate support, as being exposed can destroy credibility and cause the court to rely on your spouse's numbers for your own income, expenses, and valuations. One housewife who lost credibility claimed a gasoline expense for her car that was so high, it would only be remotely possible if she drove more than a long-haul trucker. Another husband claimed to be spending a small fortune on vacation travel while in the middle of the COVID lockdown. There are people who will claim $100,000 a year for pet expenses by doing things like renting a horse stall from their own stabling company at several times the market rate. Spouses routinely overstate spending on food that would overfeed a family four or five times their size. On the other side of the equation, one spouse tried to set an artificially low standard of living during the intact marriage to influence findings about need claimed—despite having a million-dollar and growing wine collection—to be spending a comparatively small $1,000 monthly on food and drink, meaning this person's claim would only work by having started buying wine before being born.

It is not uncommon to see the obvious manipulations by spouses who suddenly begin making large contributions to their employer-sponsored retirement programs. It is one thing if the contributions were historically made, but another thing to begin this practice shortly before or during the divorce. Omitting bonuses or extra sources of income are other common yet costly mistakes to the spouse's credibility once discovered.

Be aware that sometimes a person will purposefully overestimate or underestimate an asset as a litigation strategy, but this can also backfire when the asset gets distributed to the wrong party than the strategizing spouse intended. As will be discussed in Chapter 19, generally the judge will divide the assets and liabilities so the husband and wife each get an overall 50% from the marriage. A case in point concerned Donald, who valued his wife's diamond ring at three times what she had valued it on their financial affidavits. During the trial, it was obvious the judge had a credibility issue with Donald. His intention was to try and trick the judge into distributing the ring to his wife at a grossly inflated value so that he would receive a greater effective share of the marital assets. Instead of awarding the ring to the wife, the court awarded the ring to Donald at *his* valuation in the equitable distribution schedule of the final judgment. Donald had outsmarted himself!

It is important to know your affidavit's numbers during deposition and especially at trial. In one case, after the attorneys each questioned the wife at trial, the judge began asking questions about her testimony regarding approximately $150,000 she claimed to have spent during the divorce. However, her affidavit did not support the lifestyle claimed. The transcript contained question after question by the judge, and the wife's credibility diminished with each answer she gave. We have also seen transcripts where a party claimed to have no knowledge whatsoever of their own expenses and wanted to rely on their accountant's figures. This tactic does not always work, as judges can disbelieve the ignorance and choose to use the other spouse's explanation.

Unfortunately, being accurate in the moment can also be problematic when the primary income earner is starving out the other spouse who is temporarily spending almost nothing because there is no money coming in. Such spouses will rarely switch to the path of brazen deficit spending to maintain a "reasonable" lifestyle given the circumstances and accruing debt while complaining to the court and requesting temporary alimony. Instead, these people normally end up listing the presently reduced spending as if those were normal numbers for their expenses, which has negative consequences. First, the court could take those numbers at face value and set the poorer spouse's needs far below the real amount. Second, testifying on the stand about the "real" expenses when money is verifiably not being spent is going to result in that testimony getting picked apart, with the spouse portrayed as a liar. The solution to escape this problem is to fill out the affidavit with the present spending *and* a second column of what the expenses would reasonably be but for the bad acts of the other spouse.

Sometimes we even suggest a third column, which would reflect a more accurate lifestyle after marriage. For example, a marital home the parties sold that had larger attendant expenses would be replaced after the divorce by a smaller home with less expensive upkeep, although right now the spouse rents a cheap apartment. Better divorce attorneys like to use endnotes next to a particular category listed on the financial affidavit because it allows for greater explanation as to the dollar value used.

In summary, when filling out your affidavit, be sure to include all assets and liabilities. Be as accurate as possible when listing your income, expenses, and valuations, and be able to back them all up with appropriate documentation.

THE MARITAL RESIDENCE—STAY, LEAVE, OR SELL?

"There's no place like home."[51] That phrase still rings true. But for many couples in the throes of divorce, the reality of home will change. The physical residence they lived in now brings the dilemma of whether one spouse should buy out the other spouse and stay or whether the parties should just sell the marital residence. If you are facing this issue, there are factors to consider to help you determine your best option.

REASONS TO STAY DURING YOUR DIVORCE PROCEEDINGS

Your situation may not be able to afford two households during the dissolution litigation, where one spouse stays and the other moves out. Of course, the best chance of success is for two spouses to put aside their differences while living in the same house or at least tolerate each other. This option becomes much more difficult if there are aggravating circumstances. You certainly don't want to end up like Michael Douglas and Kathleen Turner in the movie *The War of the Roses*!

It may be beneficial for at least one spouse to stay in the marital residence if the market is experiencing a downturn. If you can hold out until the market turns, you have a much better opportunity of making a greater profit on its sale.

You may have concerns about having equal time-sharing with your children. If you have children, you should seriously consider not moving out before having a temporary parenting plan, or at least a temporary written time-sharing/visitation agreement, worked out prior to leaving. Without this in place, preferably by a court order, you risk the chance of having less time with your children if you are out of the house and being at the whim of your spouse who remains in the home with the children. If that situation persists for a significant period of time as the status quo, the judge may continue it indefinitely.

You may have concerns about losing personal property. Once a spouse moves out, there is a real and proven concern that cherished heirlooms and valuable personal property, like jewelry, will vanish. Your spouse may even claim the items in question never existed! One way to overcome this result is to take a comprehensive inventory, ideally with a time-stamped video, as well as pictures of the home's furnishings and the personal property of the parties. This will provide you with a tangible record of your belongings to prove the existence of these items during your divorce proceedings. You may want to take your jewelry, as well as any special heirlooms, to another location. They could be put in a safety deposit box or left with a family member or close friend for safekeeping.

REASONS TO TEMPORARILY LEAVE THE HOUSE

There is increased fighting and contentiousness that is not only hard on you, but hard on your children.

You may want to have your own space at this time.

You are concerned your spouse may try to create a negative impression of you with the court by seeking an injunction or restraining order against you, by calling the police and claiming you caused your spouse to fear for their safety or caused some physical altercation. This could not only result in your arrest, but if a restraining order is in place, you may be ordered not to come within 500 feet of your home, and time-sharing/visitation with your children may be severely limited or allowed only with supervision.

REASONS TO KEEP YOUR HOME AFTER THE DIVORCE

You want to permanently live in the home, or at least live there until the children are no longer minors. Make sure you consider all the financial and emotional factors before making this decision. The first question to ask yourself is if you can still afford the home post-divorce. The cost of a home is much more than just the mortgage and its interest rate. You should talk to a real estate broker, your insurance agent, and a financial planner. What are the real estate taxes, and are there homeowner association or condominium association dues? Are there any community assessments that will be sought in the near future? What will homeowners insurance cost? In Florida, the cost of insuring a home is very different than insuring the same sized or priced home in Ohio. Does the home need a new roof to maintain your insurance? How old is the air conditioner or heater? Will any appliances need replacement?

You want to keep the house to use the property for investment purposes.

OBTAINING SOLE TITLE TO THE HOME

Presuming the title is not already in your name alone, you will need to buy out your spouse's interest in the property. Most often, this can be accomplished as part of the equitable distribution—for example, you get the home and your spouse gets other assets that equal the net value (the found fair market price minus debts like a mortgage or credit line). Of course, if the home is encumbered with a mortgage or some other debt, you will almost certainly need to pay off or refinance that debt as part of the divorce. Just from the perspective of fairness and equity, keeping your spouse on the hook for a debt on what is now your property is these days treated as unfair and inequitable. In fact, your Final Judgment may have a clause that orders your spouse's name to be removed from the debt within a fairly short amount of time or the home will still be ordered to be sold.

Even if you can immediately pay off the home's debt, you might want to keep it because of how mortgages and other debts can affect alimony. Should you be seeking alimony (either for a large number of years or permanent), then because keeping this debt on the home increases your expenses, it also increases your reasonable monthly needs on which alimony is based.[52] A comparison needs to be done between how much you expect to earn from investing the money that could pay off the home's debt, as that income might decrease your alimony, versus how much more alimony you would receive by continuing to carry the debt. But this is not a straight comparison of interest earned on investments versus interest paid on the mortgage. Remember, payments on debts like mortgages are also normally a mix of interest and principal. Provided you are not too greedy about doing this, alimony could well subsidize the principal portion in addition to the interest portion of your payments and make it much easier to keep the home. Keep in mind that 30-year mortgages are far more common than 15-year mortgages and being too obvious about wanting this alimony-based subsidy will hurt your credibility.

This occurred in a case where Nancy used $100,000 from her $370,000 share of the marital home sale proceeds towards buying a new home and put the remaining $270,000 into a money market fund. Although the marital home had carried a 30-year mortgage, with the balance of $220,000, Nancy financed the $320,000 cost of her new residence with a 15-year mortgage, making the new home's mortgage payments approximately the same as the mortgage had been on the marital home. Had she taken a 30-year loan rather than a 15-year loan, her payments would have been $1,200 instead of $2,500 monthly. During an appeal, Nancy argued she needed the full alimony the trial judge had awarded to her to cover her mortgage. However, the appellate court found that the only reason Nancy's expenses were not substantially less was because instead of applying the proceeds of the sale of the marital home to her new residence, she invested it. The appellate court also stated she allowed her monthly payment to nearly double by obtaining a 15-year mortgage instead of a 30-year mortgage, so the alimony payments she received would completely pay for her new home by the time her husband retired. The appellate court reversed the trial court's order, with instructions for the judge to consider Nancy's decrease in expenses resulting from the sale of the marital home.[53] The same reasoning would apply in pushing to have an accelerated repayment of a credit line compared to the basic repayment schedule.

Should there be a debt you need take your spouse's name off of, then depending on the type of debt, multiple means may be available to you. However, the three things that will matter most are your credit quality, your income, and your other debts.

Your credit rating will increase or decrease the cost of any newly issued debt based on how good or bad the rating. The better your credit, the lower the interest rate you will be offered; the worse your credit, the higher the interest rate, if you get offered a rate at all.

No matter how good of an interest rate you might qualify for, you will need a certain amount of income to be deemed capable of actually paying the debt in a reliable manner. Obviously, the greater the debt, the greater the income that is needed to pay it. In addition to your wages or salary, there are other types of income that can qualify: investment income; regular alimony and child support payments for the most recent three months (though some loan funders will have differing requirements); income from a trust that is at least twelve months old (again, some institutions will have different requirements) where you have also received at least one payment prior to closing and were not the grantor of the trust;[54] and regular gift payments given to you by parents, other relatives, or a very good friend. The long and short of this is that you must be able to produce documents that will show there should be no concern about your income being able to cover servicing the debt.

Since many people have more than one debt at a time, these other debts are also considered by the lender. The percentage of your monthly income from all sources that pays your other debts is your debt-to-income ratio. You need to consider what counts as debt for this ratio and what does not. Most types of debt count: revolving accounts like the monthly minimum for a credit card; lease payments (with an odd exception for certain types of solar panels); student loan payments (and that can include forbearance pauses in payment); time-share loans (but not necessarily the maintenance fees); installment payment agreements with the IRS; monthly payments for other real property; car payments; your monthly housing expense, which aggregates property taxes, insurance, and homeowners association dues; and any other debt the loan originator believes is appropriate.

Other debts will not need to be considered at all, at the lender's discretion. The first big category is that the loan originator might not consider any debt for which your remaining repayment time is ten months or less. Debt assigned by court order, such as your name on the car loan for your spouse's car, can potentially be excluded. Should you be self-employed, then your debts that have been routinely paid by the business for at least twelve months could be excluded. Debts issued by a financial institution and tied to investments that can be readily liquidated to pay off that debt, like margin borrowing on stocks, can also be excluded; however, there is a very big exception, as of this writing, regarding borrowings tied to cryptocurrency. There are contingent liabilities that you agreed to, like an adult child's student loan, that could be excluded from your debt ratio. Finally, if for some reason a third party independently and directly pays one of your debts, like a relative paying your car note, the loan originator might be persuaded to exclude this debt as well.

Even with all that in order, the type of loan you will be taking matters. For those who have VA loans, the VA might allow you to directly assume the existing loan. If the existing loan is at a lower rate than what you could currently get by refinancing, it will generally be much better to attempt to assume the loan rather than get a new one. Moreover, assuming an existing loan means taking it on at the present stage of its amortization, which is the debt payment's split between principal and interest. The farther you are into a loan's repayment period, the greater the percentage of the payment is applied to principal, increasing your equity in the property. Other institutions will likely be far less willing to allow loan assumption. A new loan, which includes a refinancing, means restarting the amortization schedule and shifting most of your early payments to interest rather than principal.

When loan assumption is not available, the question becomes rate and term refinance or a cash-out refinance. The main difference between the two is that cash-out refinancing will come at a higher rate.

Yes, this is a lot to consider. It is also why you need to have your financial affidavit and the rest of your finances in order to properly deal with what is likely one of the largest and most impactful debts following your divorce.

REASONS TO SELL YOUR HOME

There is a robust market. The market conditions make it advantageous to sell because you will be able to get top dollar for your home.

You are unable to afford two households. You and your spouse cannot keep the marital home and purchase a second home after the divorce. By selling your marital residence, you both may have the ability to purchase less expensive homes or rent with the division of surplus equity.

In Florida, if the house was owned prior to the marriage but has a mortgage that is paid with marital funds, from the date of the marriage to the date of filing, the spouse who did not own the house can still get a portion of the value by which the house appreciated. If the house was owned free and clear by your spouse before marriage, but after the marriage there were additional rooms, a new pool, a refurbished kitchen, or other significant improvements made with marital funds, the improvements are marital.

The situation often arises where one spouse, the spouse who usually is living in the marital residence, is resistant to selling the house, even when there is a court order directing its sale. We have seen a number of actions taken to drag out this process. They include:

- Not agreeing on a listing agent.
- Not agreeing to a listing price.
- Not allowing the house to be shown or allowing it shown only at inconvenient times.
- Not maintaining the yard so the grass and landscaping becomes unkempt.
- Allowing the pool to turn green.
- Keeping the interior of the house a mess.
- Not fixing leaks or making other necessary repairs.
- Letting mold grow in the house.

Some of these issues can be remedied before they have a chance to occur. For example, the court order may state that if the parties cannot agree on a listing agent, then each of them will choose a listing agent and the two listing agents will select a third agent who will be the listing agent for the property. If the parties cannot agree on a price, the order can require the listing agent to set the price, and if it doesn't sell within a certain time period, the parties can negotiate for a new listing price. You really don't want the house to sit on the market for a long period of time or for it to be advertised as a sale for a couple in an impending or recent divorce, because this encourages lowball offers. If the yard and home are beginning to lapse into disrepair, your attorney can seek a court order to cure this. However, we have generally seen that the fight becomes about who is required to initially pay for the upkeep and repairs, as the order may have only addressed how the expenses for upkeep are split from the profit made once the house is sold. If the house sells for substantially less than it could have but for one spouse dragging out the process so the home no longer is selling in an up-market, or due to the degenerated condition of the house being caused by one spouse, then the court can consider the dissipation of this marital asset against the spouse that caused the delay or was responsible for the home's upkeep.[55]

Lastly, how is the personal property divided between the parties? Sometimes the process can be easier with some forethought. However, it is usually an emotional process, and can be purposely conducted in a way to hurt the other spouse.

When dividing the items in their home, Jessica decided she wanted the living room and dining room furniture. Knowing her husband, Earl, when they began dividing up the furniture, Jessica suggested that they start with the family room. Earl told Jessica he wanted the family room furniture. She next suggested the master bedroom. He wanted that furniture and the furniture in the guest rooms. Earl didn't care about the furniture in their children's bedrooms. However, when she next suggested the breakfast room, he also wanted that furniture. When they had divided up all the furniture in the house except for the living and dining room, Jessica told him that since he had chosen most of the furniture in the house, she should at least get the furniture in the living and dining rooms. Earl agreed, feeling like he had won this battle. It had taken less than ten minutes to divide up all the furniture in the house. They made a list of which furniture each had chosen, and both signed and dated this list.

However, dividing up the rest of the household items was not as easy. Jessica and Earl couldn't agree on which pictures and knickknacks each was entitled to, as well as who got the dishes, silverware, glasses, serving pieces, pots and pans, towels, and so forth. They decided the best option was to group each category of items in a written list, and then Earl and Jessica would take turns choosing which item they wanted, which would be reflected on the list they both would sign and date. Where it was agreed certain items were owned by a spouse prior to the marriage or were given specifically to one of the spouses during the marriage, those items would remain with the intended spouse and were listed as such. If there were items of disputed ownership, they were to be put aside, to be later fought over in court or to have a special magistrate appointed to rule if no agreement could be reached.

During the selection process, Jessica quickly came to realize Earl was choosing items he really didn't care about but knew she treasured. This was emotionally painful for her, but she did not want to escalate the process by choosing items that were important to him, because she knew he would end the selection process in anger, and they would be spending a significant amount of money they didn't have to fight about it in court. She instead selected items important to her when it was her turn to choose. The division of their marital personal property took the couple many hours to complete, and in the end, Earl was fighting Jessica over taking one more toothbrush from a package of seven toothbrushes purchased from a discount store, though this was still better than needlessly fighting in court.

We have seen court cases where the litigants spend thousands of dollars fighting over lightbulbs and lawn chairs. If the personal property is unable to be resolved, the parties' affidavits will usually have a space for them to list the value of different types of personal property.

Don't be surprised if the household items are not worth what you initially paid for them. The court will look at what they can be sold for today as used furnishings. Your full house of furniture may have cost you $75,000, but it may only be worth $7,500 for purposes of estimating its value at the time of your divorce.

One last suggestion: if you are contemplating selling the house, you should definitely plan on dividing the household items prior to the house being listed. You don't want to be caught in the situation of having to decide and them move out all your possessions on the day before the closing, which has a tendency to arrive before the parties have had a chance to take care of this, especially in high-conflict divorces when one or both parties are procrastinating during what could be a painful process. In the end, if you and your spouse are able to settle your personal property issues timely, and without court intervention, you will be way ahead of the game.

CHAPTER 17

BUSINESS INTERESTS—HOW THEY ARE VALUED

EVEN MORE SO THAN THE MARITAL HOME, A BUSINESS CAN BE ONE OF, IF not the most, valuable assets in the marriage. How a business is valued and who gets the business can therefore have a very significant impact on property division/equitable distribution, alimony, and child support.

When it comes to jointly owned businesses, at least in Florida, there is a strong drive to have the parties no longer be in business together after the divorce. The act of compelling former spouses to remain in business together brings about an intolerable situation.[56]

It is not expected that parties can successfully stay in business together after a divorce. The reasoning behind that principle is simple. Very few spouses can continue working together in the same closely held business while getting divorced, and remaining functional together afterward is a near impossibility.[57] Even just giving one former spouse a share of the profits is often too problematic.

Would you trust your spouse during, and especially after, the divorce to ensure the business keeps running smoothly? If your spouse has one or more other businesses, what is to stop your spouse from letting the one you still have an interest in wither from neglect? Some former spouses might purposefully cause a business to fail out of sheer spite or a scorched-earth desire, just to see the other side have less. An owner can use all sorts of ways to ensure a fully functioning and theoretically profitable business has very little or nothing left over for a monthly/

quarterly/yearly income-based payment to a former spouse. Maybe now is the time for new equipment, or a new roof, or a new parking lot, or a remodel that besides making the business look better will ensure compliance with all the latest local, state, and federal operating codes. There can always be something to eat up income rather than make that money available so a former spouse can pay personal bills. Sometimes this process is purposefully dragged out to starve a former spouse of funds and force sale to the managing former spouse for pennies on the dollar. To prevent any of this from happening, it is far better to have the spouse who can best use the business take ownership at whatever value the business is worth.

Calculating the value of the business is therefore of vital importance. A business owner, with no other special expertise beyond being an owner, can testify as to the value of that business, but it is usually far better, when possible, to hire an independent, third-party valuation expert. In general, the same considerations given to hiring a divorce lawyer, as discussed in Chapter 4, apply to picking a valuation expert. Make sure the intended expert has appropriate credentials and familiarity with the type of business to be valued and that they are a good fit with you.

There are three main approaches to valuing a business: market, income, and asset.

MARKET APPROACH

If there are enough other similar businesses as the one at issue in your divorce, an expert may base a valuation on comparable other businesses, just as real estate appraisers can determine a value for your home based on other similar homes in the area. For this to be a valid method, there needs to be more than just a lot of businesses in your area; these businesses also need to be sold often enough to create a pattern. For example, if you own a car wash business with a conveyer belt washer, then even if there are a dozen or more car wash locations in your area, one or more of those other business would need to have traded hands in the last several years to establish a market for what a comparable business has sold for. Even for something as common as a restaurant franchise, other types of restaurants can have very dissimilar values, such as a McDonald's versus a Subway versus a Domino's Pizza.

INCOME APPROACH

This method figures out how much a business earns in a given timeframe (usually a year), and then a "multiplier" is determined and multiplied against the business's income to derive the value of the business. For many businesses, the most straightforward method is to calculate the Earnings Before Interest, Taxes, Depreciation, and Amortization (aka EBITDA). Earnings equate to all the money coming in less all of the business's expenses other than what is considered the "expense" of amortizing assets, by deducting value each year over the long term (usually for tax purposes), depreciating assets (again usually for tax purposes), and the amount the business actually pays for income taxes. Those three expense items do not count under EBITDA, but everything else like rent, leases, mortgages, material costs, utilities, shipping costs, and of course wages and salaries are all factored in to find the Earnings in EBITDA, which becomes the business's income.

However, in many smaller and family businesses, a lot of what would otherwise be left as earnings gets expensed as the owner's salary and benefits. In situations where the owner's salary blurs into profits, then a similar method called Seller's Discretionary Earnings (SDE) can readily be used instead. The final value of a beauty supply business owned by a wife going through divorce was worth either $210,000 based on her expert's valuation of the business and considering her salary, or it was worth $550,000 based on the husband's expert's consideration of her salary. The trial judge had the discretion to, and did, pick the wife's valuation.[58]

Once the amount for earnings is found, then comes the multiplier, which is the real secret sauce. The multiplier number can vary widely from industry to industry and even business to business within a given industry. A business with earnings of $250,000 and a multiplier of 3 would have a value of $750,000, but that same business with a multiplier of 7 would instead be valued at $1,750,000. Whether that multiplier is 2x or 22x or something else entirely will come down to what your expert can convince the court is reasonable for your specific business.

ASSET APPROACH

This method adds up the values of all the individual assets in the business and subtracts the liabilities. Any asset that can be readily sold has value and must be valued from land and buildings, to inventory, to raw materials, to furniture, to tools, to office equipment, to patents, to cash in the bank account, to accounts receivable, along with anything else. After that, subtracting all the debts the business has will give a baseline value for the business.[59] Yet, many businesses are sold for more than just the baseline net value, and the term for this difference is called "goodwill." Just like how a multiplier is added to the income valuation approach, goodwill is that something extra that increases the value for an asset valuation approach and will also be established on whatever your expert can convince the court is reasonable.

There is an extra wrinkle with goodwill. In Florida, for divorce purposes, there are two types of goodwill, personal and enterprise. The portion of goodwill that would remain with the business even if the owner spouse were no longer a part of it is enterprise goodwill, while the rest is personal. Enterprise goodwill counts as part of the business value for consideration as a marital asset, while personal goodwill does not. As an example, patrons of a restaurant chain probably do not care much that the owner spouse happens to have an ownership interest in the franchise at issue and will keep eating at the location whether or not the owner spouse continues to be involved. Conversely, a restaurant named after the owner who is the cook, controls the recipes, and is really the only reason why people dine there is going to have almost total personal goodwill.

This is also a very common situation with professional service businesses. One trial court valued an insurance business that a husband took over from his father as being worth over $10,000,000, based heavily on enterprise goodwill. That judgment was reversed, with all the goodwill treated as personal due to the personal relationships in maintaining sixty important customer accounts, and the value of the business dropped to under $3,000,000 for the business's hard assets.[60]

OTHER DISCOUNTS AND ENHANCEMENTS TO BUSINESS VALUATION

Having a minority ownership stake can incur a valuation discount. Should there be five equal 20% owners, then the spouse's share of the business should be worth 20% of the appraised value. However, if the other four owners would be absolutely hostile to a replacement investor, that 20% share is going to be worth less.[61] Conversely, if the owning spouse tends to be the tiebreaker in votes as to how the business is run, then those specific shares would be worth more than the shares held by the other four owners. For a concrete example, one appellate court reversed a judgment that did not apply a marketability discount to a husband's 33% share of his family's business when the value of that business would affect his ability to pay alimony.[62]

An industry-wide boom or slump is going to affect value. A turnkey business where the new owner can just slide right in and immediately begin earning is going to be more valuable than one that will take a while to build an established, reliable client base. Something else to consider is that being tied to a small number or one major client can be a blessing that enhances value or a curse that diminishes it.

Your expert's methodology, not just in which valuation approach was chosen but in all the work that went into following that approach and the reasons for doing so, becomes the information the expert will present to the court. Your spouse can have his or her own expert present a competing valuation. At that point, it becomes a duel between the experts through the questions asked by each side's lawyers and the answers given by the experts. The duel will attempt to promote the positives of each side's method and reasoning while highlighting the flaws and unreasonability of the opponent's process and conclusion.[63] Your jurisdiction might allow the judge to pick one side or the other or do something along the lines of splitting the difference. At least in Florida, the judge cannot split the difference between the two sides, so the final judgment of dissolution will have findings of fact that almost always come from the more credible side.[64] On those occasions when the court finds both sides lack credibility, in Florida, the judge must still set a valuation, supported by the facts of the case, with the starting point being the value from the side that was less unbelievable.

WHO GETS THE FAMILY PET?

IN MANY HOUSEHOLDS, A PET IS CONSIDERED PART OF THE FAMILY.[65] Americans spent $130.8 billion on their animals in 2022, according to the Bureau of Labor Statistics.[66] What happens to your precious pet when there is a divorce? How will the judge rule? It depends on where you live! Some jurisdictions' decisions are determined by property law, while others are guided by laws and decisions that look to the well-being of the pet.

JURISDICTIONS USING A PERSONAL PROPERTY ANALYSIS

It may surprise you to learn that although you may think of your pet as a family member, in some jurisdictions, pets are personal property and are subject to equitable distribution, with an economic valuation like pots and pans or a lamp.[67] Unless the pet is a pedigree, or has some other special quality, the pet may be considered to have very little economic value, despite being so personally invaluable to its owner. In Florida, pets are personal property, not subject to custody or visitation.[68] The courts, already overburdened and understaffed, are clogged with cases concerning children's issues arising after the final judgment has been entered, and so courts want to have finality when it comes to decisions concerning pets. After the final judgment is entered, courts don't want the additional burden and unlimited drain on judicial resources required to address such issues as failing to follow an order for a pet's visitation schedule between the former spouses.[69]

If the pet was purchased by one spouse prior to the marriage, it will be considered that spouse's nonmarital personal property, even if the other spouse took care of the pet during the marriage. The pet may also be the property of one spouse if given as a gift, inherited, or purchased with nonmarital funds. In Scott's divorce action, the court awarded him a dog as nonmarital property. The dog was in the custody of his then-wife, Lizabeth, at the time the final judgment was entered. However, she refused to return the dog to him. Scott filed a motion for contempt against Lizabeth and sought to enforce the final judgment for his dog. The trial court judge refused to hold Lizabeth in contempt, and instead of her returning the dog, Scott got the dog's fair market value. The appellate court reversed this decision, not for a personal reason, but because the dog was Scott's nonmarital property.[70]

When Hala and Mohamed were divorcing, they were able to resolve most of their issues with a marital settlement agreement, except who would keep the two dogs, Liberty and Nico, which both parties believed were bonded to each other and should not be separated. Hala claimed she took care of the dogs from the time the family adopted them in 2013 and 2014, respectively, to the time the parties separated in 2017, and Mohamed cared for them thereafter, which was three years by the time of trial. Hala testified Liberty was adopted to be her emotional support dog and was her constant companion. She argued justice required the judge to award an emotional support animal to her. The court pointed out that in Florida, emotional support animals are typically given special consideration under the law, but the judge found Hala did not have a physical or mental disability requiring an emotional support animal, and she only proved Liberty provided emotional comfort, as would any ordinary pet.[71] The court also took into consideration that the children, who lived the majority of the time with Mohamed, were comforted by the dogs throughout the dissolution proceedings. Both dogs were awarded to Mohamed.

Pets that are fought over during divorce litigation don't necessarily have to be cats or dogs. At the marital home, Louise had six chickens that she named, raised, and cared for as her pets since they were day-old chicks. While getting divorced, Louise's estranged husband, Earl, cared for them when she traveled for her job. At one point while Louise was away, he moved the chickens to another location and refused to reveal their specific whereabouts despite Louise's repeated requests, leaving her devastated.

At a hearing, she requested the court order Earl to tell her where her pets were located so she could get them back. Earl's attorney argued the chickens were just like any other asset and Louise had not asked for advanced equitable distribution to be awarded them. If she claimed he had dissipated this property, then the court could value the chickens, and for $10 she could get a couple more chicks. Earl told the court the chickens were in a beautiful place, but he could not remember the location. Although it was clear Earl had given away Louise's chickens to hurt her, the court determined it lacked the ability to grant Louise any relief. Fortunately, Louise was ultimately able to independently locate and retrieve her pets.

JURISDICTIONS CONSIDERING THE ANIMAL'S WELL-BEING

Some jurisdictions still consider pets as property but view them differently than other personal property and seek to provide them with protections in law, such as prohibitions on animal cruelty or looking at their best interests, which wouldn't apply to miscellaneous personal property. If you are in a jurisdiction that takes this approach, the following cases may act as a guide for the standards the courts sometimes apply and the issues you can raise to provide you with a better chance of being awarded custody of your pet. For example, a court in Tennessee considered the needs of the parties' dogs and the ability of the parties to care for them when awarding the dogs to the husband.[72]

A Vermont court recognized that although pets are property, they are different from other property, as the pets are alive and form emotional attachments with their owners that run in both directions. Although in most cases they have little or no market value, pets frequently become close companions and an important part of the daily life for countless owners. That court found either party would provide the dog with a good life, and the parties had a temporary agreement to share their time with the dog, but the court explained it could not enforce an agreement for visitation or custody for animals and must assign the pet to one party. The factors the judge considered in making this decision were the dog's welfare and its emotional relationship with the parties.[73]

During David and Tina's divorce trial, a Michigan court heard testimony from David that he was interested in being awarded only the dog, Finn, as he was not interested in the parties' other animals. The judge expressly acknowledged that the dog was personal property, but rather than treating Finn as chattel for property division, the court applied a best interest standard and awarded the dog to Tina so all the animals would continue to stay together.[74]

For many years, the New York courts generally viewed pets as any other type of personal property and applied traditional property law to disputes regarding ownership. However, as a result of a 1999 case involving a cat, and the 2013 custody fight by two spouses over their dog, the New York courts began using the "best for all concerned" standard when deciding pet ownership cases.[75] In accordance with that standard, each side would have the opportunity to prove not only why each would benefit from having the animal in their life but why the animal had a better chance of living, prospering, loving, and being loved in the care of one spouse as opposed to the other.[76] Another major development later occurred with the passage of a statute codifying the requirement that a court must consider a companion animal's "best interest" when awarding possession in a divorce or separation proceeding.[77]

If you live in Illinois or Alaska, these states have statutes that permit, upon divorce, joint ownership of the animal, with the court taking into consideration the animal's well-being.[78] Under this criteria, a wife was awarded the parties' German shepherd when the court noted the husband placed his own interests over the dog's well-being.[79] California has a statute for the care and ownership of a pet that provides when there is a divorce, the court may assign sole or joint ownership of the pet, taking into consideration the pet's care.[80] This care includes, but is not limited to, the prevention of acts of harm or cruelty and the provision of food, water, veterinary care, and safe and protected shelter.[81]

IN SUMMARY

It is vital for you to know the law in your jurisdiction so you can provide the most compelling evidence to be awarded custody or sole ownership of your pet. In addition to the cases discussed in this chapter, which have included various arguments made by the parties in seeking the award of their pet, the following is a checklist of factors the judge may consider:

- Whether the animal was purchased before or during the marriage.
- Whether one spouse technically owns the pet to the exclusion of the other spouse.
- Whether one spouse was primarily responsible for the pet's physical care, including but not limited to, feeding, walking, grooming, and veterinarian visits.
- Whether one spouse was financially responsible for the pet's care.
- Whether either spouse mistreated the pet.
- Which spouse will have primary custody of the children, whether the children are involved in caring for the animal, and the nature of their attachment to the animal.
- Which spouse will have possession of the other pets, if any.
- Whether one spouse's lifestyle is more compatible with pet ownership.

- The pet's age and physical health.
- Whether there are other pets involved, and whether it would serve the best interest of all involved to keep the animals together in one home.
- The parties' ages and physical health.
- Whether one spouse's residential situation would expose the pet to danger of some sort.
- Whether the pet might present a danger to persons or other pets at one spouse's residence. [82]

For many families, pets are the equivalent of children and are to be loved and protected. One way to help avoid fighting over the animal in the future is to have a written agreement that spells out what would happen to the pet should the parties divorce.

DIVISION OF OTHER PROPERTIES AND OF MARITAL LIABILITIES

SOME SPOUSES STAY IN AN UNHAPPY MARRIAGE, THINKING THAT IF THEY outlive their husband or wife, they will get everything. However, in Florida, if your spouse cuts you out of his or her will, you will only be entitled to 30% of the estate as your elective share. If you divorce, the court usually provides for a 50/50 split of "marital" property as that is the starting point for an "equitable" distribution of assets, unless there is a reason to depart from that. Cynical as that is, you may actually receive more of a distribution if you leave rather than stay!

Remember, marital property is equitably divided, while nonmarital remains the separate property of the spouse who brought it into the marriage, inherited it, was specially gifted it, or acquired the property through trading other nonmarital marital property. Some jurisdictions also consider as nonmarital any assets and liabilities acquired after the petition for marital dissolution is filed. Your jurisdiction might handle matters differently, but in Florida, the moment that petition is filed, all newly acquired assets and liabilities become separate property of the spouse who acquired them. Therefore, another reason somebody might plan for a divorce is because of an intent to start a business without wanting to risk sharing the rapid expected increase in the value of the intended business.

The first thing to keep in mind about equitably dividing marital assets is that while the term "splitting" is often used, that does not mean literally dividing in half every asset that can be split. Instead, it means getting half the overall net value. If there is $200,000 in total assets and $50,000 in debt, then each spouse will walk away from the marriage with $75,000 worth of net value. The math breaks down as $200,000 in assets minus $50,000 liabilities for net equity of $150,000, which then gets halved. Now, that might be split with each spouse getting $100,000 worth of stuff and $25,000 in debts, but it could just as easily be one spouse getting all $50,000 in debt and $125,000 in assets while the other spouse gets $75,000, or some division in between. Because equitable distribution rarely ends up being able to divide all the assets and liabilities with no remainder, the leftover amount to reach a 50/50 split tends to be called a balancing payment, an equalization payment, or a similar name. Again, this only applies to marital items; one spouse could have over $10,000,000 in nonmarital assets, but if the marriage has net assets worth a comparatively smaller $150,000, then that $150,000 is all that gets split, unless your jurisdiction has some law that states otherwise. However, that nonmarital $10,000,000 could still affect matters like alimony, child support, and payment of attorney's fees.

Next, the idea of property subject to equitable distribution is exceptionally broad. If the item has value and is marital, then it should be named and included for equitable distribution. Think of more than just bank accounts, investment accounts, vehicles, the marital home, and other real estate. There was just a whole chapter on businesses. Furniture bought during the marriage should be valued and distributed, but furniture each spouse brings into the marriage remains separate property, and yes, courts have been reversed for forgetting that fact.[83] A garage full of tools, even used ones, can pile into sizable value, but like with furniture may readily have a significant amount of nonmarital items that need to be separated out for valuation in distribution.[84] Cryptocurrency has "currency" as part of its name, with various coins and tokens trading for exceptionally large sums of money, warranting inclusion on a distribution schedule.[85] Airline miles and loyalty points from a credit card, a chain store, or a hotel, and other sources all have value,[86] as do collections of personal property, whether that be stamps, cards, coins, guns,[87] clothing, or anything else. Valuable wine has been ordered distributed as well as liquidated[88] to further equitable distribution. Paintings, sculpture,[89] and other art is generally valuable to somebody, sometimes extremely valuable, and should be included. Club memberships and time-shares can have a sizeable value.[90] Animals, whether for the farm or ranch like horses[91] and cows to family pets should be included.[92]

There are intangible types of property such as patents,[93] licenses, copyrights, trademarks, and royalty rights. Something as unusual sounding as a capital loss carryover (the remaining unused losses that did not offset capital gains) can lower a spouse's tax payments in future years and so are worth distributing. A tax refund itself, normally from the last year (or partial year) of the marriage can be an item that should be distributed rather than just letting one spouse take the whole refund without comment. Settlements of various types—such as those from a former employer or the proceeds of a personal injury suit—are also distributable. Though depending on the jurisdiction, that might include the full value of the settlement or, as in Florida, lost wages and earning capacity along with reimbursement spent on medical bills is marital, but not pain and suffering awards which are nonmarital.[94]

The fact that the above nonexclusive list did not include jewelry was purposeful. Yes, jewelry is of course an asset class that definitely warrants inclusion on an equitable distribution schedule, especially watches, necklaces, bracelets, and other adornments. Engagement rings, however, are a little special in that unless your jurisdiction has law finding otherwise, these are nonmarital property and should be carved out separately from the rest of any jewelry for valuation.[95] In one case, a husband's own lawyer admitted in trial that the wife's $10,000 worth of jewelry included a $4,000 engagement ring. Because the final judgment left the valuation at the full $10,000, following an appeal, the case was remanded for the husband to pay an additional $2,000 in equitable distribution equalization for half the value of the ring that was nonmarital.[96] The reasoning is straightforward, as the ring or rings being offered are done in contemplation of marriage, since the couple is not actually married yet.

So long as somebody, somewhere, would be willing to pay a reasonable price for the item in question, include it on the equitable distribution schedule. Moreover, for property that has little value, also called nominal value, but that you want to ensure gets distributed fairly, put it on the schedule.

The opposite side of assets, for valuation purposes, is liabilities, as indicated in the sample distribution of assets and liabilities above. Any form of debt accrued during the marriage—whether a mortgage or a vehicle loan, medical debt, student loans, credit card balances, or anything of negative value—goes on the schedule.

A spouse might attempt to remove assets from the marriage by putting them into a trust. However, in jurisdictions like Florida, it can be possible to have the full value of the property moved into a trust still be included for equitable distribution. When one husband moved $250,000 of marital money into a revocable trust, that money retained its marital character and was subject to distribution.[97] In another case, a wife moved almost $4,000,000 into a revocable trust the year before filing for divorce, and then in the middle of the marital dissolution, moved that money into an irrevocable trust, with herself as the trust's beneficiary. While the irrevocable trust is technically and legally a third party, with those assets no longer being owned by the husband or the wife, the trial court could still consider the improper transfer and treat the wife, for distribution purposes, as if she personally kept all that money.[98]

That money was moved into an irrevocable trust brings up another point to consider: Make sure to add relevant third parties like trusts and businesses to the marital dissolution action if those entities potentially control assets that will have a real impact on your equitable distribution. One example of this would be the many spouses whose "personal" car is in fact owned by a closely held family business. Unless that spouse is also getting the business, extra steps would be required to keep the car. Generally, a court cannot order a party who is not part of the litigation to do something. Now, if the other spouse is going to be the 100% shareholder of the business post-dissolution, the court could order the other spouse to direct the business to properly retitle the car. But what happens when the business-owning spouse is not the sole owner? It is probably easier to just have the business be included in the dissolution, so the court can order the distribution directly, and leave it to the spouse dealing with the business to reimburse the business for the value of the vehicle.

During the marriage, how property is titled, whether jointly or in one spouse's sole name, is not automatically determinative of the asset being marital or nonmarital. The default stance is that anything acquired during the marriage is marital. Similarly, when nonmarital assets are mixed together with marital assets, the assets tend to be considered "comingled," and what was once nonmarital instead becomes marital. If one spouse had a nonmarital account but that account then became the main account where both spouses deposited their paychecks and it was used to pay marital bills, all the original value left in that account would probably be treated as marital. The same can happen when a person suddenly comes into a large sum of money, like by selling a separately owned home or bunch of stocks, and dumps all the proceeds into an already marital account, where it sits and some gets used for marital purposes.[99] Contrast that with titled property like land, which generally takes some explicit, overt effort to shed nonmarital character.

All of these situations are rebuttable where arguments can be raised that there was never an intention to make some property marital, and if the asset can be properly traced then the item at issue might still be found to retain its nonmarital character. However, the more that is done, the harder it tends to become to prove the asset remains nonmarital. One wife put $50,000 of her nonmarital money into a certificate of deposit titled jointly as husband and wife. When the CD matured, the wife had it reissued alone in her name. Because that wife convinced the court the only reason the CD was jointly titled was for testamentary purposes with no intent to make a gift, the money was treated as nonmarital.[100] Another wife, Maria, inherited about $2,000,000 and moved $1,000,000 into a marital account, where the money sat untouched for nearly the remaining entirety of the parties' marriage. Even though shortly before the parties filed for divorce, Maria made some personal loans using the money in the marital account; she was still able to prove to the court that the money could be properly traced as being hers right down to the deposits matching the repayments on those personal loans.[101]

This process can get trickier when it comes to a signing bonus, stock options, or other large employment related payouts or promises of payment that happen after the filing of the petition. The question becomes whether this money is being paid in advance for future work or for work that was done before the petition. Benefits already earned are marital, but payments for future efforts to be performed post-petition are nonmarital. For the husband who was awarded stock options each year he worked for a company, even those awarded options not yet vested were treated as marital property.[102] Conversely, another husband was promised a significant amount of stock options as a signing bonus, but a percentage of those options were only transferred after each year of work; the still outstanding unvested options that were contingent on still working with the company were treated as nonmarital because those would only be awarded for future work.[103]

Other assets are potentially very easy to recognize as nonmarital. The biggest category is probably inheritances made from a deceased relative to only one spouse, followed by gifts from others to just one spouse, as well as interspousal gifts with the intent of making that property belong solely to one person. The money a wife inherited that was left in an untouched and not comingled account was her separate nonmarital property.[104] A mother made a series of gifts to her married daughter, totaling over $800,000, for the purpose of investment. After making the initial investments, the daughter did not touch the money, so when she later got divorced, the original gift and all the appreciation (that approximately doubled the investment's original value) were all nonmarital.[105] When a wife gave her husband 500 shares in a business, complete with having her accountant testify to the business's board this was a gift, those shares in the eventual divorce were determined to be the husband's separate property.[106] Conversely, when a husband received money from his father's trust that was used to buy a boat, the boat ended up being classified as marital, because the money did not go directly to the boat manufacturer; instead, those funds first went into a marital account, where comingled money was also used to pay marital bills.[107] Clearly, the most important factor for these sorts of assets to be classified as nonmarital is to be kept separate.

Assets—especially real estate, retirement accounts, and businesses—can end up in a mixed state, where the underlying ownership remains entirely (or partially, in the case of retirement accounts) nonmarital, while a small to large percentage of the asset's overall value is considered marital. Think about the housing market; over time, when the values of all the other houses in your neighborhood are going up, your home is probably increasing in value as well. If nothing else is at issue for a nonmarital house worth $250,000 at the start of the marriage and is currently worth $750,000, then the whole of that appreciation is normally nonmarital. For a house that was worth $500,000 at the start of the marriage, promptly underwent a $50,000 remodel with marital money, and was sold as soon as the remodeling was done for a net of $550,000 (after brokerage fees and all other expenses), that $50,000 increase in value is likely to be marital as active appreciation. Combining the two examples, consider a nonmarital house worth $500,000 that gets a $50,000 expansion paid with marital funds and is sold several years later for $1,100,000. The original $50,000 in marital value would apply, and a good argument could be made for another $50,000. However, if a real estate appraiser opines the house would have netted a sale of $1,200,000 or $1,300,000 had a less "unique" remodel been done, then extra appreciation beyond the original marital money spent is probably not going to be awarded, and some portion of the original $50,000 spent remodeling might be at risk as having not improved the property's value.

The full or partial repayment of mortgages, credit lines, and other debts impinging on property can also convert some nonmarital value into marital value (and some jurisdictions might consider that process as more than merely gaining value but a transition to an actual ownership stake). Continuing with the same $500,000 house, if it came into the marriage with a $300,000 outstanding mortgage balance and after the mortgage was paid down by $100,000, then provided there is no other appreciation, the marital value component would be $100,000. Had the house increased in value to $900,000 by the time of the divorce, that same $100,000 would normally be worth $180,000. Were the mortgage to be paid off during the marriage, then at a $900,000 value, most—i.e., $540,000 of the value ($300,000 pay-down + $240,000 appreciation)—would be marital.

When there are multiple debts taken out at different times, some of which have been partially or fully paid off, some of which have been refinanced, and some of which fluctuate like a credit line, pinning down the most accurate amount of appreciation can rapidly become more complicated. Further, debt repayment based appreciation can also interact with asset improvement based appreciation. For example, a home might have a mortgage and then the married couple uses marital money to do a home remodel, whether paid out of current savings or by taking out a home equity credit line that is later repaid with marital earnings. This is again why it is very important to have an appropriate financial expert assist in your divorce planning and the divorce itself when warranted.

A home was chosen for these examples as hopefully being easier to comprehend, since mortgages and remodeling tend to go with homes, and homes tend to appreciate in value over time. This can apply to practically any asset. Closely held businesses are not static assets; somebody started or bought in, and there is ongoing management and reinvestment to consider. Trading on an investment account to grow its value and margin borrowing is a mix of both effort and debt. The restoration of a classic car or a work of art can have both active and passive appreciation aspects. Fixing up a condo and then renting it out counts. Improvements to a farm, ranch, timberland, or similar income-producing piece of property also count. Day-trading to grow a stock portfolio probably means all of those gains from the first day of trading during the marriage and onward will be marital. Shifting responsibility to an investment manager is a mixed bag, since the level of communication between investor and manager (including the manager's independent decision-making) as well as the receptiveness of the judge will impact the extent to which that can be considered not contributing labor.

If a nonmarital asset is more valuable now than when the marriage started, and neither you nor your spouse did anything to cause that increase in value, then all the value remains nonmarital. The more effort and the more money expended on that asset, the more of the value increase is likely to be deemed marital. This can even include paying property taxes and for substantial maintenance that prevents the asset from being lost. Note, there are jurisdictions, like Florida, where this applies to the marital effort expended by either spouse during the intact marriage, not just the effort of the spouse seeking a piece of the value. Paying off a mortgage with paychecks from either spouse counts toward value. When restoring an object, the labor expended can easily end up counting for more than the cost of materials or parts. Efforts by either spouse toward growing a business can make marital some or all of the gains in value not tied toward personal goodwill. Salesmanship done during a marriage that increases the value of property, like getting music licensed for commercials or movies, is going to make at least some of the increased value of that property marital. Consider your situation and make the arguments based on the facts and circumstances to support reasonable arguments maximizing the marital component of any nonmarital property that is not yours and minimizing the marital value portion of your nonmarital property.

That being said, nonmarital retirement accounts and pensions that are passively handled by the owning spouse tend to end up being distributed in a somewhat different manner. If you came into a marriage with seven years toward a pension, earned another twelve years during the marriage, and it took another year post-petition to get divorced, then the seven years before and one year after are your nonmarital pension, but those middle twelve years, representing 12/20ths of the pension are marital. When the distribution schedule is prepared, you can expect that pension to be divided into 14/20ths for you (7/20 + 1/20 + (12/2)/20 = 14/20ths) and 6/20ths to your now-ex. Should a person enter into a marriage with a retirement account and grow it during the marriage only through work-related contributions, with all the rest of the gains coming from passive management, the retirement account will likely be divided up similarly to a pension. The fractional percentage tied to contributions made before the marriage remains nonmarital, contributions made during the marriage (and their associated appreciation) are marital, and contributions made post-petition are nonmarital. Active trading in the retirement account or borrowing against the account during the intact marriage may have appreciation related repercussions during the divorce. Hopefully, you have kept the statement (or can get a reprint) from as close as possible to the date you got married showing the value of these and any other accounts.

Pensions and retirement accounts may have rules about dividing them, preventing private retitling part of the asset from one spouse to another. By the same token, attempting to do any sort of cash-out or withdrawal from an account, but especially an account with lots of unrealized gains or in a tax-deferred account, to satisfy equitable distribution should probably be avoided in most circumstances, except in those rare instances where you purposefully want a large tax bill. Instead, request your judge split the asset through the entry of a Qualified Domestic Relations Order (QDRO). The purpose of a QDRO is to appropriately divide the associated asset by court order without disturbing the contents of that asset. A pension manager will properly split a pension in response to a QDRO and ensure the eventual payments go where they are supposed to. Transferring or dividing an investment account by QDRO is a nontaxable event, so neither spouse will be paying taxes on gains or losses simply to move the money. None of the assets in the account are liquidated or sold and repurchased for the new owner; the ordered percentage is moved intact. Afterward, following the divorce, the tax consequences only start affecting a former spouse owning the divided account once that divided piece incurs realized gains or losses.

Throughout this chapter, the term "value" has been used numerous times, and examples of values have been given without explaining how to value an asset. As blunt as it sounds, the "how" is however you, and your valuation experts, can convince the trial court. No singular, set-in-stone method works for every asset in every situation. There are chapters in this book dedicated to businesses (which themselves have multiple valuation methods) and the marital home, and here are many other types of property to think about.

Consider all of your jewelry, however much or little that might be— what is it worth right now? If you took it to a jeweler, would you get original retail price for each piece? Are some items more valuable? Are some items less? Would it average out to retail or something different? Would those values change at auction or is the likely buyer a pawnshop or metals dealer? What about all the art you own—did somebody get discovered? Do you know (or can you hire) any experts who can give an opinion?

For a car, truck, SUV, or other road-going vehicle, do you use Blue Book value? How about Black Book? You could have the car appraised by an online service. A local or national dealership could appraise the vehicle for cash or give a different number for trade-in. Maybe there is a specialist to render an opinion because there is something special about that vehicle. The same can be said for boats and planes.

Think of all the furniture you owned before getting married and that was acquired during the marriage. What would it be reasonably worth, and what method did you use to come to that value? Are there any antiques? What about musical instruments? There are various collections people can own. What are items in your collections being sold for in nearby stores and online marketplaces? What is the worth of a monetized viral video on a streaming platform? When it comes to any asset worth the expense of doing so, have a relevant appraiser give the asset a review.

Literally any and all property—whether real, tangible personal, or intangible—can be valued and, depending on your circumstances, potentially should be valued. For any property you personally own or control, you can give the court your opinion as to its value, and this is treated as evidence. A trial court erred in accepting the testimony of a husband as to the wife's jewelry without appropriate evidence to support his valuation, just as it was improper to include the value of her gold coins that he speculated she had, but which he never counted.[108] For anything where there's even a slim chance of a fight over valuation, you will likely want—or possibly need—an expert who can provide a probative, supportable opinion to the court.

When it comes to valuation, words like "supportable" and "reasonable" are vitally important. Getting too greedy in overvaluing or undervaluing assets is likely to backfire. More than just losing credibility with the court, your equitable distribution schedule has a real likelihood of finding the intentionally misvalued assets added to the wrong party's side in distribution. Did you claim to value all the furniture in the house at just $1? If so, be prepared for your ex to be awarded ownership of all of it at that absurdly low number. Perhaps you valued some rust bucket of a car with over 200,000 miles on the odometer, bald tires, and a cracked engine block that not even a junkyard would take as being worth $30,000. Then congratulations, and have fun driving your $30,000 car . . . once you get that engine replaced.

From a similar perspective, trial courts are not supposed to enhance the value of an object in equitable distribution for sentimental reasons because that would place an inappropriate priority on an asset in place of financial fairness to the other spouse.[109] The good china brought over with some relative generations ago is worth no more than what a willing buyer would pay for the collection. The first wooden table you built, breaking your arm harvesting the lumber, is worth no more than an equivalent table made with the same type of wood along with the same level of craftsmanship and name recognition.

However, a trial court can consider sentimentality when determining who gets awarded a marital asset, like that china, that table, or in some jurisdictions, the family pet.[110] Still, pushing the judge for an asset means you could be stuck with that asset irrespective of the consequences. When a husband repeatedly pressured the court for restricted stock in a dry-cleaning business he wanted to expand, he got those shares, and although his business partners tried to defraud him of those same shares, the appellate court would not offer him relief from the judgment.[111]

The date on which an asset or liability is valued also matters. Depending on your jurisdiction, the trial court does not need to use the same valuation date for all assets and liabilities. Each and every item can, in theory, have a different valuation. Provided the evidence supports using different dates for different items, the judge has the discretion to pick multiple dates. If your divorce looks like it could take many months, or possibly multiple years, do you want to have the marital home valued as of the date the petition is filed or some later date based on the real estate market? A recently purchased used truck might be worth less than the loan on it, but over time, paying down the loan could leave the vehicle with positive equity, even accounting for ongoing depreciation. The value of a stock portfolio can vary from day to day, and cryptocurrencies from moment to moment. More importantly, should you need to tap into a bank account to pay routine bills and reasonable living expenses during the divorce, causing the value of the account to drop, then it would normally be inequitable to use the balance on the date of the petition rather than the date of trial.[112] When was the balance on a student loan last updated for a financial affidavit? Is one spouse newly carrying a larger credit card balance than in the past? Any one of this sampling of items can have a real impact on the equitable distribution in a divorce. What might, on paper, look like a 50/50 asset value split could, through the use of alternative dates, be in reality close to 60/40 or 70/30.

Carefully choosing which assets to take in distribution is the other major means of structuring an equitable distribution that gives the appearance of being 50/50 but which instead is going to have outsized inequality in the real world. Take the hypothetical of a spouse who, during the marriage, begins a new job offering temporarily restricted company stock options and a 401(k). If that 401(k) has been fairing very mediocre in the market, with nearly all growth from employer contributions, while the stock options will probably triple in value or more, offering to QDRO the whole 401(k) earned to date rather than splitting both the stock and the account 50/50 could be advantageous. The spouse keeping the options will gain all that appreciation down the line should the stock increase in value as expected, while the spouse with the 401(k) will later need to deal with all the tax implications of withdrawals from a tax-deferred account. A less extreme example would be a married couple with two nearly new cars: one of which is leased, while the other has no car loan or a very small one. Distributing the leased car to the spouse requesting alimony also means acknowledging the spouse having increased "need" for alimony based on the expense of the lease payment, while distributing the owned car means both little to no car payment for alimony needs calculations and simultaneously having an asset almost certain to depreciate in value post-dissolution.

Should you have any concerns that the structure of who gets which assets and liabilities would become unfair, you must present appropriate evidence to the trial court.[113] After all the assets and liabilities were divided up between Christina and William, he was going to make an equalization payment to her, and he chose an account with a tax advantage, which Christina argued on appeal would result in an inequitable distribution because the tax consequences had not been properly factored. Yes, the failure to consider tax consequences could place the dissolution judgment out of compliance with the equitable distribution statute in that jurisdiction, but since neither side presented evidence about tax consequences, it was too late to complain on appeal. Under most circumstances, a judge cannot be faulted for failing to consider an issue unless the judge is made aware of the issue and probative evidence is presented.

A party can end up being imputed the value of assets that no longer exist or are no longer in their possession through the "theory of dissipation." This has also been alternatively called "depletion" and "diminishment." Unfortunately, those same three D-words have also been interchangeably used to describe spending money on reasonable living expenses, as well as innocent loss of value through no fault of either spouse. The specific requirements vary by jurisdiction, with Florida, for example, generally considering only dissipation post-petition and within two years of the dissolution petition being filed, unless equity and justice so requires going back more than that time. Having an affair is the most classic example of dissipation, and this can readily include money spent on the "paramour" during the whole course of the divorce. Claude's affair with a mistress overseas eventually carried quite the price tag.[114] His wife, Hala, initially thought at least $150,000 had been spent. When the court eventually found the amount to be $383,551.83, Claude was charged with the full total in equitable distribution. There are jurisdictions that, for equitable distribution purposes, only consider the money dissipated pursuing adultery and not the act itself, as one wife engaged in three affairs while married, but as no money was traced as being spent on her affairs, there was no change to the distribution of assets.[115]

Selling a vehicle to a friend of a relative for well below market value just to shrink the size of the marital estate could end with the value of that vehicle being treated as yours for equitable distribution purposes.[116] Given certain circumstances, the money that came from the husband's settlement with a former employer, which a wife spent during a divorce on cosmetic surgery in Beverly Hills, was dissipation, but not the portion of those funds used to pay health insurance and home utility bills.[117] Drug use can be another good reason to support dissipation, and one appellate court reversed a trial court with instructions to include all marital assets for distribution, including those dissipated by the husband on drugs.[118] Gambling is another cause for dissipation. In a pair of cases,[119] one wife was awarded an effectively larger share of the marital estate because money the husband gambled was treated as dissipated, but another wife was not able to claim any part of the $90,000 her husband lost in the two years leading up to the divorce because, while she might have disapproved, she gambled as well. Further, the husband in the second case had the additional cover for his activities, as the gambling was done to entertain business clients and therefore had a marital purpose.

As can be seen from these various examples, money spent (including assets liquidated) on matters unrelated to a marriage, particularly when the marriage is undergoing a breakdown, are funds that can be added back to the spender's side of an equitable distribution schedule, provided the spouse was unaware of or strongly objected to the spending. The net effect of doing so results in half the value (presuming a 50/50 distribution split) of the dissipated assets going to the non-dissipating spouse. Were there $160,000 in assets, that would be split $80,000 and $80,000 in value, but had there been $20,000 in dissipation, the marital estate would be treated as if it had $180,000 in value. One spouse would be awarded $90,000 in assets, and the other would receive $70,000, because of being assigned the $20,000 of marital assets that spouse had dissipated.

Forging a spouse's name to a debt can be treated like the inverse of dissipation, where depending on the jurisdiction the debt incurred by forgery is made outright the nonmarital debt of the forger.[120] Instead of the debt making the net value of the marital estate smaller and the spouse who receives a marital debt having other assets distributed to offset this, making the debt nonmarital foists the entirety of the negative value to the forger without any corresponding offset. Consider a marital estate with $120,000 in assets and a $50,000 indivisible debt. Under normal circumstances, one spouse might receive $85,000 in assets along with the full $50,000 debt, while the other receives $35,000 in assets—effectively splitting the negative value of the debt equally, even though only one spouse assumes responsibility for it. Were the debt revealed to be a forgery, the assets would be split $60,000 and $60,000, with the forger separately assigned the $50,000 as nonmarital debt.

To the extent that you are concerned assets could wind up being dissipated during an upcoming or ongoing divorce, ask the court for an injunction to freeze the use of most assets. That way, an order of the court would be required to spend marital money and sell off marital assets. Your court may even have a local rule that automatically puts in place orders forbidding asset dissipation.

Dissipation and valuation tactics are not the only ways to get more than half of the available assets. A spouse can always just outright ask for a larger share by requesting an unequal (though still equitable) distribution. Provided you have a compelling reason to seek more than half the value of the marital estate, request the court award the increased amount and make sure the court details adequate findings to support the award in the final judgment. Failure to make the appropriate findings is ready grounds for reversal, despite having facts in a divorce that might have easily supported an unequal award.[121] Some jurisdictions might treat the potentially distributable value in a nonmarital asset as needing to be requested in the form of special equity or an unequal distribution rather than an arguable component of the regular equitable distribution of the marital estate.

The simple fact that you happened to contribute most of the money to purchase a marital asset is not, in and of itself, generally a good enough reason to get additional value back during divorce, unless your case is in an exceptionally lenient jurisdiction. To push that argument, far more information and more compelling evidence needs to be proven, like in the case of Florence and Yves.[122] Shortly after getting married, the couple decided to build a home in Florida, but not long before the home was completed, Yves wanted to back out, and he was living elsewhere with another woman at the time. His name was not on the deed. Although Yves did live in the home for about two years, he then moved out and remained in a separate residence for another seven years when Florence filed for divorce. Florence was the only spouse who paid all the bills for the home, attended to all the upkeep, and all the repairs for those full nine years without a single contribution from Yves, who was not there for most of that time. The requested unequal distribution was not for all of the home's value but for the increase in value that accrued after Yves left. Conversely in another case, a wife wanted an unequal distribution of the marital home's value because her father had paid off the mortgage; the denial of her request was readily affirmed on appeal.[123]

Distribution of debts rather than assets can also be requested to create an unequal equitable distribution. Because a husband ousted the wife from the marital home, forced her to rent a place elsewhere, and then rented out part of the home to third parties while keeping all of the rent for himself, it was appropriate to unequally distribute all the mortgage on the marital home to him.[124] Student loan debt incurred during the marriage is no different from other marital debt, even though the education purchased through that debt benefits one person. A judge's decision was reversed for attempting to unequally divide the entirety of a student loan debt to Brenda when Thomas's only argument was he did not benefit.[125]

A request for control of a child's college savings plan to make sure the other spouse does not liquidate it can be reason for unequal distribution for that account.[126]

In the middle of one divorce, a wife destroyed the husband's collection of books, Star Wars toys, and sports memorabilia.[127] The trial court awarded the husband unequal distribution due to the wife's conduct. But the need for appropriate findings again matters. The appellate court allowed for an unequal distribution, yet found the evidence did not support unequally distributing well over $100,000 from a retirement account to cover this damage; the husband had valued his collection at $14,500 on a financial affidavit and that was the point for valuation unless on remand the trial court wanted to take more evidence.

Even in jurisdictions that would treat dissipation under the umbrella of an unequal distribution, the direct transfer of funds or assets in an unequal distribution can have double the impact compared to treating dissipated funds as if that was still part of the marital estate. Using the example of the $14,000 in destroyed collectibles in a hypothetical $200,000 marital estate, as "dissipation" that would make the estate worth $214,000 and be split as $107,000 to one spouse and the other would have $93,000 + $14,000 dissipated, while a direct transfer would leave the martial estate at $200,000 and result in a split of $114,000 to $86,000.

In more unusual cases, there can be advantages to having an unequal distribution, where you purposefully take less than half of the marital estate. Remember, alimony is generally based on "need" and ability to pay. By giving the other side more assets, especially in a lump sum, the other spouse has less need for alimony. Continuing with the post-judgment interest example above, $250,000 might be "worth," at 6%, $15,000 a year of imputed investment income for a lifetime alimony award. Were alimony likely to be awarded for 10 years, the same $250,000 could be worth the equivalent of $30,000 to $35,000 or more of "need" reduction. Arguments can be made that by having the extra funds up-front, the other spouse might not need a car loan or would have a much smaller mortgage. Also, there are other things that could be done rather than sticking that money under the mattress to be doled out in one-tenth increments each year. If the "need" for alimony is eliminated, then in jurisdictions such as Florida, there would be no alimony award in the first place. While alimony might be modifiable in amount or duration down the line, once alimony is eliminated, some jurisdictions will not allow a former spouse to ask for it later, post-dissolution. By the same token, the swing in equitable distribution can affect both sides' incomes for child support calculation purposes. This path is more likely to come about by settlement agreement, but it is something that can be presented in argument to the trial court.

One more thing to make sure of during your divorce is, if at all possible, do not have any money or assets you are taking be classified as an interim or an advance equitable distribution. Mentioned multiple times through this chapter is the concept that assets used to pay reasonable living expenses and spent in furtherance of the marriage (even the marriage in breakdown) will not usually count toward equitable distribution, though this may vary by jurisdiction. If a marriage had $100,000 in net assets just before the dissolution petition was filed and by the time of the final hearing only $30,000 was left, even though nobody actively engaged in dissipation and there were no significant drops in market value, then each spouse will get $15,000. Instead, had one spouse requested an interim equitable distribution of

$20,000, the marital estate would be treated as worth $50,000, constituting $30,000 remaining + the $20,000 previously distributed, and the spouse with the interim distribution would only be walking away with $5,000 out of that remaining $30,000, having already received $20,000 as an advance distribution.

After you have figured out the content of your equitable distribution, the next step in the process is actually getting it distributed. As indicated above, trial courts have the power to order the property of parties before the court be retitled as needed (within certain limits for nonmarital property, depending on jurisdiction) to effectuate distribution. Refinancing is often required for titled property, such as real estate and vehicles, in order to complete the distribution. The note holders for these types of assets are normally unwilling to simply assent to swapping borrowers or relieving one borrower spouse from liability on the loan. When the spouse who would be distributed an asset has bad enough credit, has a bad debt-to-income ratio, or outright lacks the income to maintain the asset post-judgment, that asset may well be ordered sold in the judgment.

For any property in which you have shared ownership interest, whether as tenants by the entirety or the tiniest sliver of actual ownership through being a tenant in common, you can always request the court order the property be partitioned, which means publicly sold unless the other owner(s) buy you out at fair market value. The failure of a trial court to rule on a requested claim for partition is reversible error.[128] Businesses and real property are the most frequently partitioned items, but any asset can be subject to sale under this claim. Although Florida is famous for homestead protections, a successful claim for partition will lead to the home being sold. One of the few partial limitations, depending on jurisdiction, is that if a parent has majority time-sharing/custody with a child, along with exclusive use and possession of a home subject to a partition claim, then the judge may be encouraged within the law to refrain from having the home sold until the child reaches the age of majority, unless economic circumstances would make it highly inequitable to hold onto the property rather than sell it.

Following similar reasoning, major and potentially minor assets can be requested to be ordered sold, with the sales proceeds ordered to be shared based on whatever ratio works best for that specific divorce. Continuing with the same example of a $500,000 house with $200,000 left on the mortgage, should the house sell for exactly $500,000, there is potentially $300,000 (excluding sales expenses for the moment) to be divided up. The court might order that net proceeds be split 50/50, or 75/25, or 99/1, or any other ratio depending on what best fits your circumstances. The court could order that the first $50,000, or $100,000, or $250,000 of the proceeds go to one spouse, with the remainder being split in some other fashion. Having a fixed dollar interest in the sales proceeds can provide security if the actual sale price ends up falling a bit short of the appraised estimate. On the other hand, having a split of the proceeds could be extra beneficial in a hot market, where the asset eventually sells for significantly more than the appraised value.

Since there are almost certainly going to be closing costs, brokerage fees, transfer fees, and local fees and taxes, as well as possibly state and federal income taxes, you need to present to the court how those expenses are going to be paid out of the proceeds. If all the expenses, other than income taxes, are 7–8% of the sales price, then still on that $500,000 home, this would work out to $35,000 to $40,000, which is going to come out of somebody's share. Parties and the judge likely also need to consider the carrying costs of the various expenses to keep the asset in good condition (and continue making regular payments on any debt encumbering the asset) until sold. Is one side ordered to pay without reimbursement, or will the party paying some or all of these carrying costs be made whole after the sale? What is the plan in the judgment to structure priority of payments if the amount of the sale is not enough to cover both the fixed payments in equitable distribution and the carrying costs to be reimbursed before or after any fixed value payouts are covered?

Is there going to be a court-ordered time limit to get any refinancing or sale done? Should that fail to happen, will there be mandatory consequences, like relisting the asset at a lower price, which could repeatedly lower over time? Is one side or the other refusing to participate in the sale, such as by not agreeing to the listing price, signing with an appropriate (and possibly court-ordered) listing agent, or not signing the actual sales contract? Pure stubbornness by a spouse has caused more than one asset to go into disrepair or foreclosure, resulting in a much lower eventual sales price than what was originally expected in the judgment. In the event there are ancillary consequences—such as delays in obtaining your post-judgment home because the down payment was supposed to come from the sale of the marital home, and you're now facing higher interest rates—you may need to return to court to request an adjustment. This could involve modifying your distribution to allow for a larger down payment that maintains your previously expected monthly payment, or seeking a reassessment of alimony. All of these questions and concerns should be addressed with your attorney regarding any major asset with at least a moderate probability of needing to be sold as part of or immediately following a divorce. Moreover, when it comes to tax consequences, those should be considered no matter how far into the future tax issues would arise.

Equitable distribution of assets, including any equalization payment, can be ordered to occur as a lump sum within a certain period of time, or some portion of the distribution could be ordered paid out with installments over a number of months or years. Should you be the equalization payment recipient or the party who is waiting for the other side to sell at least one major asset, such that it will be some time before you have your full distribution, ask for post-judgment interest to be paid on whatever amount will not be paid immediately. Interest rates vary by time and jurisdiction, but if you are waiting on, say, $250,000 and the interest rate for your judgment is 6%, that would be $15,000 a year. Not requesting post-judgment interest, when appropriate, can mean forgoing substantial sums of additional money that could have, and should have, been awarded.

The periodic payment of equitable distribution with installments is very different from alimony. While alimony is enforceable through having a party be found in contempt of court, in many jurisdictions, the payment of equitable distribution is not. Other aspects of distribution might be enforceable by contempt. Three of the most frequent would be the judge ordering a party to relinquish property, ordering a party to sign a document like a title or a contract, and ordering a party not to interfere with attempts to reasonably sell an asset. Being held in contempt can have serious consequences, including the suspension or loss of licenses (whether for driving or for practicing certain professions) and being jailed. Getting out of contempt means complying with the purge provision in the contempt order.

However, one major limitation about contempt proceedings with fiscal elements is the requirement to find that the person being placed in contempt has the present ability to pay a given purge provision that is expressed in dollars. That can equate to an amount at issue, and on occasion is much less; moreover, the person seeking for the court to find somebody in contempt has to go through this process each time. Conversely, the main enforcement mechanism for explicitly monetary aspects of equitable distribution is to get the amount owed converted to a money judgment. After getting a money judgment, the judgment holder can execute on it, which can involve pursuing assets wherever those might be stored and having the police come out to directly seize assets (cash, cars, furniture, clothing, whatever) for later liquidation in order to satisfy the judgment. Depending on your position in the divorce, do what needs to be done to protect your assets and to take the assets to which you are entitled.

CHAPTER 20

TAX RAMIFICATIONS YOU MAY NOT HAVE THOUGHT OF

TAXES CAN PLAY A FAR LARGER ROLE IN A DIVORCE THAN MOST PEOPLE realize. A divorce is likely to be an expensive process paid for by liquidating assets, since very few people have the funds to pay from discretionary income after dealing with the normal living expenses. When these assets are sold at a profit, somebody is going to be required to pay taxes on those gains and by the same token, when an asset is sold at a loss, somebody may get to use those losses to lower an income tax burden.

This application of gains and losses is most exemplified when selling a house. The marital home is commonly sold during a divorce or ordered to be sold as part of the final judgment of divorce, unless one former spouse can readily afford to maintain it after the dissolution. While the $250,000 capital gains exclusion for singles and $500,000 exclusion for joint filers eliminates the tax burden on sale for many divorcing couples, it does not always, and remaining taxes need to be planned for and handled. Moreover, that exclusion only applies to a primary residence and then once every two years, presuming the person or couple have lived in the home, as the primary residence, for at least two of the last five years. As a related point, should one spouse move out to an owned rental property that also ends up needing to be sold, so long as that rental becomes the spouse's primary residence for two years, the other property can instead have its own $250,000 exclusion. But remember, there will be only one exclusion per person, and no more than once every two years.

The judge will need to be informed whether the exclusion applies in your case—or, if not, the reason it does not.

If it is to your advantage to do so, any reason that would minimize taxable gains resulting from an asset's sale should be brought to the court's attention. These can include major home repairs and improvements, transfer fees and taxes, broker fees, real estate agent fees, and legal expenses. Ask your accountant about what can be used for any given piece of property.

A home that has been bought, for whatever reason, just prior to somebody filing for divorce can have radically different tax consequences depending on how quickly the home is sold. After all, taxable gains from owning the home for more than a year will be taxed at long-term rates, but so will losses. The basic rate difference as of the time of this writing, without even getting into surtaxes, can mean being taxed 20% for long-term gains versus 37% for short-term gains. Should it become recognized that there will definitely be a loss from the sale, it might be better to try to have the property sold with less than a year's ownership so as to have the losses be classified as short-term losses at short-term rates. Of course, the same logic of timing a sale based on ownership length also applies to stocks, bonds, and many other types of investments.

Collectibles, which include: art; rugs and antiques; alcoholic beverages; gems, coins, stamps, and precious metals (with exceptions for certain minted gold, silver, and platinum coins along with precious metal trade bars); as well as anything deemed by the Treasury as a collectible are all taxed at a long-term gains rate that caps at 28% rather than 20%. That miscellaneous category includes items like musical instruments, historical objects and, as of this writing, NFTs.[129]

One oversized tax burden that many people fail to account for in the heat of the moment is the cost incurred when making an early withdrawal from a regular 401(k), regular IRA, SEP, and other similar tax-deferred retirement accounts, as compared to withdrawing from a non-deferred account like your basic savings or investment account. Withdrawing or liquidating a basic investment account is going to have tax implications based on the gains or losses based on the specific assets sold in that account. However, when dealing with a tax-deferred account, in addition to the ordinary income taxes incurred (which is calculated by adding the withdrawal to the top of your regular income), early withdrawals by those who are not yet 59.5 years old from a tax-deferred account will likely face an extra 10% surtax, and this adds up fast.

For one basic example, a person whose income would normally be placed in the low-end of the 22% bracket needs to withdraw $25,000 to pay expenses or due to a court order is not going to face $5,500 in additional income taxes ($25,000 x 22%) but instead ($25,000 x [22%+10%]) $8,000 in additional taxes. If that same person does not have the extra $8,000 handy to avoid an income tax shortfall, then that might require further dipping into more withdrawals from the same surtax-affected account. That $8,000 would incur a further $2,560 in taxes, and that $2,560 (if unable to be paid out of pocket) would mean another $819 in taxes, and so on. All told, and taken as a single tax-inclusive distribution from the retirement account, to net out $25,000, a person in the 22% bracket would need to take a total of *$36,764*. Rather than 22% this works out to an effective tax rate of a *whopping 47%*! These snowballing withdrawals tend to place a portion of the person's income in a higher bracket, making the total situation even worse. Scale that up to someone ordered to pay a larger lump sum of $100,000 while in the 35% tax bracket, and the taxes owed—rather than being just $32,000 or $42,000—would total approximately $81,818. This means the person would need to withdraw *$181,818* in total, resulting in an effective tax rate of almost *82%*! To the extent withdrawing money from a tax-deferred account pushes you into a higher tax bracket, those funds above the threshold of the line of the next bracket will be taxed at the commensurately rate, again including the additional withdrawals to pay the increased taxes.

Of course, these are just the basic federal income taxes; there may also be state income taxes owed on this same income. Unless specially educated, the court may not be aware of how significantly this can impact a person's finances and the total value of the marital estate. In one Florida case, the trial court's judgment was correctly found to have "grossed up" withdrawals from a 401(k) that included taxes and early withdrawal penalties.[130] Like so much else, when it is to your advantage, let the trial court know.

When possible, borrowing against a retirement account is generally preferable to an outright withdrawal.[131] The limit on borrowing if you have at least $100,000 in the account is $50,000. Should you have less than that invested, you can borrow up to either $10,000 or half the value of the account, whichever of the two figures is greater. Loans are not treated as distributions, with the associated taxes and penalties, so long as the loan is being properly repaid according to its terms. These terms normally: (1) require at least quarterly payments; (2) are limited to five years, with some exceptions; and (3) require paying interest, but at least that interest is paid back to your own retirement account rather than a third party. Breach the terms and that loan could easily wind up being classified by the IRS as a distribution, with all the heavy taxes described earlier in this chapter.

On the other hand, there are some rare circumstances where it might be better to dive in and purposefully liquidate. If you know with absolute certainty that you will be taking a distribution at some point in the near future (in the timeframe of your pre-dissolution-petition planning to within several years after getting your final judgment), then obviously you will be incurring these hefty taxes from that certain, upcoming distribution. Waiting till after the entry of the final judgment will almost always make this tax issue your sole responsibility unless the judgment specifically and specially accounts for it. But, knowing this distribution is definitely going to happen, you may have the option and opportunity to forcibly share half that tax burden with your soon-to-be former spouse, because incurring these taxes prior to the entry of the final judgment potentially puts the taxes in play as a reduction in the net value of the marital estate. You get the full benefit of paying for whatever the distributed money was used on while, for all practical purposes, dealing with half the taxes compared to taking the same distribution post-dissolution.

Stated another way, you know you are going to need $100,000 for some expense like a down payment on what will be your separate home, for expanding a business, or prepaying tuition, and this can either come from a regular investment account or the tax-deferred retirement account. Under most circumstances, you normally want to minimize your taxes by drawing on the regular investment account. Yet, sharing all the extra taxes is sometimes better than being solely responsible for them later. Like in the example above about withdrawing $100,000, would you rather be solely responsible for all of the roughly $82,000 in taxes or effectively split that 50/50 with the person who will be your ex? Afterward, you still have the regular investment account to separately use, which could potentially be taxed at a far lesser rate when making a withdrawal following the divorce.

Another matter to consider, when beneficial and allowable, is having retirement accounts, investment accounts, and other similar assets be split and transferred by a "QDRO," a Qualified Domestic Relations Order. Under normal circumstances, if you are ordered in a final judgment or related order to pay money from an account, or need money to comply with such an order and take it from the account, now being divorced, you are stuck with the tax consequences. Granted, you might be able to have the court equitably adjust matters because of these taxes, but the default position is that those taxes are your problem. The QDRO, by being a nontaxable event, means neither now-former spouse will be paying taxes just to move the account or portion of the account into the recipient's name. When a withdrawal is eventually made by the recipient, that is the person who will most likely have to deal with the resulting tax consequences.

Keep in mind that, just as it can sometimes be beneficial to intentionally incur a large tax bill early, it may not always be wise to split any and all applicable accounts via QDRO solely to push future withdrawal taxes onto your soon-to-be former spouse. Take the case of Nathaniel and Joanne. Nathaniel had a 401(k) worth about $36,000 on the date he and Joanne entered into a settlement agreement to QDRO half the account to her. By the time he actually went to get the QDRO, his now ex-wife's portion of the account grew in value from about $18,000 (half of $36,000) to over $113,000, which she got.[132] Therefore, if you have a high degree of confidence that a retirement account is going to skyrocket in value, consult with your accountant and lawyer about keeping such an account all to yourself and dealing with the present tax consequences of selling off something else so you can keep it.

Taxable losses can also have value. "Capital loss carryover," sometimes referred to as "capital loss carry forward," is a tax benefit that allows you to offset taxable gains and, if your losses exceed your gains, also offset up to $3,000[133] of ordinary income (such as wages) per year. This carryover comes from selling assets for less than the value at which you acquired them, which could be buying stock shares at $100 and selling at $90 or needing to sell off a rare guitar collection quickly but reasonably under the circumstances. To the extent that these losses exceed your gains from selling capital assets and collectibles, they carry over as a carryover. You do not need to use these carried losses all at once or as soon as applicable gains occur, as they carry over from year to year to use at your discretion until the year you die. However, there is no passing the carryover to your heirs.

Carried net operating losses is the business version of this. Some years, a business simply might not make money; other years (through the careful management of tax loopholes), a business might be treated by the IRS as having lost money regardless of how much money was actually gained. In either event, this leads to losses that can offset other income, but there are circumstances in which those losses cannot be deducted against present income. However, once able to be taken, these can radically alter a person's tax bill and so also have value.

There are various tax credits and deductions to consider. A common pair of tax credits to consider that tend to be forgotten during a divorce are the Child Tax Credit and the Child and Dependent Care Credit. For those whose incomes qualify, the Child Tax Credit is a flat tax credit per qualifying child, and the Care Credit is a tax credit that applies to a percentage of the money spent on care for up to two qualifying children or dependents so the spouse can work or look for work.

Any given child who qualifies for the Child Tax Credit can only be claimed by one parent, so choices must be made as to which parent gets to claim a given credit and when. Some parents will, during and after the divorce, split even numbers of children. Other parents will switch years on and off. Another alternative is for the working spouse or former spouse who pays the child/dependent care expenses to get that tax credit. Other couples will agree to have the credits go to whoever will get the most benefit. Also be aware that these tax credits affect net income, and thus the amount of child support as well as the need and ability to pay alimony.

Insofar as the Child and Dependent Care Credit is worth remembering, unlike so much else in a divorce, it is not something to fight over. Once legally separated, whichever parent has more overnights gets the credit, and if time-sharing is equal, whichever parent has the higher adjusted gross income gets the credit. While separated, should you file a separate tax return and live in a separate home from your spouse for at least six months a year, that home is the home of a qualifying child or dependent, and finally if you pay at least half the cost of keeping the home then you are treated for tax purpose eligibility of this one credit as if you were legally separated.

While this chapter has so far dealt with major items parties tend to overlook in divorce planning and during divorce, whether you file your taxes jointly or separately also matters. Many spouses file joint tax returns as a married pair. For some, this has advantages in larger income requirements before any of the joint money is taxed at the next higher bracket, which tends to be more practical when one spouse earns comparatively little, or is a homemaker, while the other earns much more. One spouse can have unusable or barely useable carried losses, while the other spouse has gains to be offset. There are various state and federal income-based programs, which use different larger numbers for joint versus separate filers, where joint filing allows both spouses to benefit in situations where otherwise one or both spouses might not. Even during a hostile divorce, sometimes filing jointly saves more money for the both of you compared to filing separately. You can file jointly only if still married on December 31 of that year. Some spouses will wait to file or finalize their divorce until January so as to benefit from the joint tax filing for the prior year.

For different couples, the opposite can be true, leading some spouses to decide to file separately rather than jointly. Even though the tax brackets for a married separate filer, as of the time of this writing, are half the size of the equivalent joint filer bracket, there are reasons to file separately. A separate filer may have a tax situation that qualifies for certain tax benefits that would have been unavailable or uneconomical when filing jointly, like income-based student loan repayment plans, where the lower earner has the larger student loan debt along with consideration of the student loan interest deduction income limit. As referenced above, the Child Tax Credit and the Child and Dependent Care Credit are income dependent, and getting these can be another reason to file separately. There is also the Earned Income Tax Credit to consider. A higher-earning spouse will typically push joint filers above the maximum income threshold for eligibility. However, especially when children are claimed as dependents, a lower-earning spouse filing separately may be much more likely to qualify for this credit. Consult with your accountant to see what will work best for your situation, as you can also switch from year to year whether to file jointly or separately.

Another big reason to file separately is simple suspicion that the other spouse might not be preparing an accurate tax return, with an insufficient payment. Filing separately can provide a degree of insulation from that, as you are holding yourself as a separate and hopefully honest taxpayer. The ultimate form of filing separately would be to attempt to claim innocent spouse status for one or more years. If the IRS grants a spouse this designation, all the relevant taxes become the sole responsibility of the non-innocent spouse. Contemplating this process almost certainly requires some degree of professional help to determine how likely the IRS is to issue a favorable decision. Of course, once your spouse knows you are pursuing this, you can expect the divorce to become all the more combative.

Finally, insofar as federal taxes are concerned, while alimony and child support are two of the most important financial considerations in a divorce and can have lasting effects for many years afterward, these two matters, at least at the time of this writing, do not directly affect your taxes. Child support is not deductible to the payor or taxable to the recipient. Alimony used to generally be deductible to the payor and taxable to the recipient if ordered by the court in the final judgment, but awards made after December 31, 2018, no longer qualify for that tax treatment. These payments may well have ramifications for your post-dissolution investment and employment decisions, but the payments themselves are tax independent.

That being said, the tax code change that made new alimony awards nondeductible may become a permanent change to the US tax code, or it may be allowed to sunset and alimony might regain the possibility of being deductible to the payor. In the event that happens there are some things to consider. Making alimony deductible to the payor only results in a net savings to the parties as a whole when the payor is in a higher tax bracket than the recipient because there is generally no net savings and no direct fiscal benefit to the payor if both parties are in the same bracket.

When alimony is nondeductible and nontaxable, then for the recipient to have $1,000 worth of bills covered by alimony, the payor needs to pay $1,000. When taxable to the recipient in the 22% bracket for example, covering every $1,000 in bills would require approximately $1,282 in alimony. Were the payor to be in the 35% bracket, then that $1,282 would have a functional net cost to the payor of about $833 per $1,000 in alimony, presuming the whole $1,282 could be deducted at 35%. However, were both parties to be in the 22% bracket, then to cover $1,000 in bills, approximately $1,282 in tax deductible alimony would need to be paid—and after netting for the deduction the payor would still essentially be out $1,000. Unless there was some special and beneficial program with maximum income limits that allowed for alimony deductions to count, there is not much point for the payor who is in the same bracket. Yet for the recipient, the consideration is more nuanced. On the one hand, the recipient can show a greater gross income when applying for loans and other events that may have higher income thresholds to apply or to participate, but on the other hand, is more likely to be excluded from programs with income limits.

Even when the payor wants alimony to be tax deductible (and were alimony to again become deductible), paying too much alimony in the first and/or second year compared to the second and/or third year might trigger alimony recapture. Reviving the recapture rule along with reviving the deduction and taxability of alimony would cause a portion of the otherwise deductible alimony to be added back to the payor's income when recapture applies. Like with so much else in this chapter, you will want to discuss matters with your accountant, lawyer, and any other relevant professionals.

CHAPTER 21

ALIMONY AND CHILD SUPPORT

ASIDE FROM THE DIVISION OF YOUR MARITAL ASSETS, ALIMONY AND CHILD support are the other major financial considerations in a divorce. This chapter will explain the different types of alimony and the factors used to determine child support.

FACTORS A JUDGE CONSIDERS IN AWARDING ALIMONY

Alimony is the court ordered allowance that one spouse pays to the other spouse for maintenance and support while they are separated, while they are involved in a matrimonial lawsuit, or after they are divorced; especially money that a court orders someone to pay to his or her former spouse after the marriage has ended.[134] Jurisdictions vary on the types and duration of alimony available, but generally the basis for alimony is the receiving spouse's need and the other spouse's ability to pay. The spouse seeking alimony has the initial burden to prove need and that the other can pay the requested amount. In Florida, courts look at a number of statutory factors in determining an alimony claim, which include:

- The length of the marriage.
- The standard of living during the marriage and the anticipated needs and necessities of life for each party after the final judgment is entered.
- The age, physical, and mental condition of each party.
- The resources and income of each party, including income generated from both marital and nonmarital assets.

- The earning capacities, educational levels, vocational skills, and employability of the parties, including the ability of either party to obtain the necessary skills or education to become self-supporting or to contribute to his or her self-support prior to the termination of the support, maintenance, or alimony award.
- The contribution of each party to the marriage, including but not limited to, services rendered in homemaking, child care, education, and career building of the other party.
- The responsibilities each party will have with regard to any minor children whom the parties have in common, with special consideration given to the need to care for a child with a mental or physical disability.
- Any other factor necessary for equity and justice between the parties, which may include a finding of a supportive relationship or a reasonable retirement.[135]

DIFFERENT TYPES OF ALIMONY – WHICH MAY HAVE ALTERNATIVE NAMES BASED ON JURISDICTION

Temporary Alimony

This type of alimony may be awarded to either spouse while the divorce is pending.[136] In Florida, temporary alimony need is demonstrated by the party's standard of living during the marriage.[137] Parties cannot waive temporary alimony during a divorce in Florida, even if written into a contract, though other jurisdictions can have very different rules. Florida courts have consistently determined that temporary alimony is among the areas where a judge has the broadest discretion and with which the appellate courts are very reluctant to interfere.[138]

Bridge-the-Gap Alimony

This form of alimony is used to provide needed assistance to "bridge the gap" in transitioning from married to single life, and assist the spouse with legitimate short-term needs, separate from and often supplemental to other alimony. In Florida, this form of alimony cannot exceed two years and terminates upon the death of either party or upon the remarriage of the recipient spouse. Florida's bridge-the-gap alimony is not modifiable in amount or duration.[139]

Rehabilitative Alimony

This alimony is awarded to assist a spouse in acquiring the education or training required to find employment outside the home so they can reenter the workforce and become self-supporting. Usually, this alimony is awarded to someone who was a homemaker, needs training to acquire a new skill, or needs additional schooling to attain a degree or credits to reactivate a former profession. In Florida, rehabilitative alimony requires providing the court with a detailed, concrete plan, including a timeframe for completion. Florida's rehabilitative alimony may not exceed five years (though the time may vary in other jurisdictions).[140] If the spouse seeking rehabilitative alimony presents a plan premised on completing a vocational or degree program, this alimony's duration should allow for completing the program.

Rehabilitative alimony may be modified or terminated in Florida, based upon a substantial change in circumstances, noncompliance with the rehabilitative plan presented to the judge, or early completion of the plan.[141]

Dana sought rehabilitative alimony to complete a paralegal training program she claimed would enable her to earn an income to help her approach the lifestyle Dana and her husband enjoyed during their marriage. When the judge only provided for paralegal training for one year, Dana appealed the judgment. The appellate court reversed that judgment, explaining that Dana's husband had the ability to pay for the full term of her paralegal training, and directed the trial judge to revise the duration of Dana's rehabilitative alimony.[142]

Durational Alimony

The purpose of durational alimony is to provide a former spouse with economic assistance for a set period of time following the marriage. Different jurisdictions can have wildly different rules, by statute or case law, as to the requirements to ask for durational alimony and for how long it can last. These rules can and do change. When it was first enacted by statute in Florida in 2010, under that name, durational alimony could not exceed the length of the marriage. The most recent version of the 2023 Florida Statute completely overhauled the length of time a party can receive durational alimony and method for computing it. However, in Florida and some other jurisdictions, durational alimony still terminates upon the death of either party or upon the receiving former spouse getting married. This type of alimony can be modified as to the payment amount, and sometimes the duration, unless a contractual settlement agreement makes it non-modifiable or your jurisdiction disallows modifications.

Permanent Alimony

Some jurisdictions have permanent alimony, and Florida used to award it in many divorce cases involving long-term marriages, after specific statutory factors were met. There can also be rebuttable presumptions for or against permanent alimony based on the length of the marriage, with certain exceptions in those jurisdictions with this alimony. With this form of alimony, the spouse receives periodic payments without a set durational time limit until the death of either party or the remarriage of the recipient spouse. This type of alimony can be modified as to the payment amount, unless a contractual settlement agreement makes it non-modifiable or your jurisdiction disallows modifications.

Some spouses believe they can live with a new partner without getting married and still receive alimony. However, many jurisdictions have enacted statutes that permit alimony to be modified or terminated if the spouse is in a supportive relationship.

Lump Sum Alimony

This is usually a fixed liquidated amount of money that one spouse is required to pay to the other spouse. Payment can be made in one "lump sum" or a defined series of payments. Lump sum alimony differs from durational and permanent alimony in that it vests immediately upon the divorce judgment, so it is not normally subject to being modified.

Lump sum alimony occasionally gets mixed up with equitable distribution. The line can get further blurred when property, like the marital home, is awarded as lump sum alimony. At a glance, lump sum alimony and equitable distribution appear to reach the same end result by moving money or property to one spouse at the end of a marriage, but the two are fundamentally different. Equitable distribution is strictly about dividing marital assets and liabilities, while lump sum alimony is about ensuring support for the recipient spouse through a single, or series, of lump transfers from the payor. Moreover, the enforcement mechanisms are different: equitable distribution is handled via execution of a judgment, while lump sum alimony (like other alimony) is enforced through the obligated party being held in contempt of court, which can include being sent to jail. Some spouses request, and some judges try to reclassify, what should be equitable distribution as lump sum alimony for this enforcement purpose. However, unless the lump award can be shown to be based on a supportive need for alimony, it is subject to reversal on appeal.

Nominal Alimony

This is an unofficial term for being awarded a tiny amount of alimony, usually durational or permanent, with the intent of preserving the ability to modify the award later. Jurisdictions like Florida do not allow former spouses to come back to court after a marital dissolution is completely over and done to ask for an initial award of alimony. Yet, there are situations where one spouse has a real need but the other spouse presently cannot pay. Therefore, having an award as small as

$1 monthly allows the recipient spouse to eventually ask for a larger award if there is still a need once the would-be payor has a better ability to pay.

As an example of several types of alimony, including a judge misnaming some, look at the divorce of Stephany and John. They were married for over thirteen years, and had two children, ages 6 and 10, when Stephany filed for marital dissolution, seeking temporary, permanent, and lump sum alimony. Stephany was a high school graduate, with two years of college and worked as a flight attendant until her first child was born. Since then, she had been a stay-at-home mom. John was employed by a major airline as a captain. During the divorce proceedings, the parties sold their home and split the proceeds.

At the final hearing, the trial court denied Stephany's request for permanent alimony. The judge concluded she made a conscious decision not to work and that she was capable of becoming self-sufficient. The judgment stated "the Wife has chosen not to work during the 2½ years this action was pending and has not put forth any plan of rehabilitation apparently believing that would force this Court to give her an award of permanent alimony. This game of judicial 'chicken' will not be rewarded."[143] The court ordered only bridge-the-gap alimony in the form of lump sum alimony, in the amount of $48,000 payable at the rate of $2,000 over 24 months, stating "the only 'gap' to be bridged was created by the Wife's refusal to move on with her life after the filing of the dissolution action." "Frankly, the Court would not award any alimony but for the generous concession by the Husband."[144]

Stephany appealed, and the appellate court reversed the judgment, finding she should not have had to use her assets from the house sale to pay for her support. The appellate court found the trial judge abused his discretion in denying her temporary alimony and directed the judge to award Stephany temporary alimony retroactive to the date she first filed her motion for temporary support. The appellate court also reversed the denial of permanent alimony, finding that even if she became gainfully employed, Stephany's needs would not be met, John had the ability to pay alimony, and the trial court's bridge-the-gap award by way of lump sum demonstrated the judge did not consider the various statutory factors necessary to arrive at a proper determination.

When it comes to determining alimony, a court may impute income (treat this hypothetical money as if it were actually being earned) where a spouse is willfully earning less and has the capacity to earn more.[145] Potential employment income is sometimes determined by hiring a vocational expert to testify to the amount of earnings and types of jobs a spouse is capable of holding, by considering the spouse's work history, occupational qualifications, and the prevailing earnings in the community for those jobs. To impute employment income in some jurisdictions, it is unnecessary to prove a specific employer would actually hire the spouse.[146]

Florida courts have also recognized that self-employed spouses, in contrast to salaried employees, have the ability to control and regulate their incomes so that their tax returns, business records, and testimony at deposition or at a hearing may not reflect true earnings. If it appears a self-employed spouse is underreporting income, the judge can impute more.[147]

Be aware that promising a spouse will never have to work again while they are married does not guarantee that spouse still won't need to work post-divorce. A judge found an agreement made during the marriage that the wife would be a stay-at-home mom and homeschool the children would not remain in effect after the parties separated.[148]

Income can be imputed from other sources besides work. This can potentially include cash left sitting in an account rather than being invested, properties left unrented (or rented below market rate), to nearly any other investment, including money tied up in a 401(k) or IRA.

CHILD SUPPORT

For purposes of child support in the United States, the age of majority to no longer be considered a minor ranges from 18 to 21. Some jurisdictions have short extensions for finishing high school or even college after reaching majority. In certain jurisdictions, support can also extend into adulthood if the child is sufficiently disabled or will otherwise need extended care as an adult. Like with so much in this chapter, consult your lawyer about the specific facts of your situation compared to the law in your jurisdiction.

Many jurisdictions, including Florida, determine child support based upon fixed statutory guidelines and calculations. The calculations usually start with each spouse's gross income, which can include many varied sources that were previously detailed in Chapter 14's income sources list.

Florida imputes income to an unemployed or underemployed parent if the court finds this was voluntary, absent also finding physical or mental incapacity or other circumstances over which the parent has no control. However, the court can refuse to impute income to a parent if the court finds it is particularly necessary for that parent to stay home with the child who is the subject of a child support calculation.

In order to determine each parent's net monthly income for child support, they can subtract allowable deductions from their gross income so long as supporting evidence for the deduction is provided.[149] Though what qualifies for deduction varies based on jurisdiction, in Florida, allowable deductions include:

(a) Federal, state, and local income tax deductions, adjusted for actual filing status and allowable dependents and income tax liabilities.

(b) Federal insurance contributions or self-employment tax.

(c) Mandatory union dues.

(d) Mandatory retirement payments.

(e) Health insurance payments, excluding payments for coverage of the minor child.

(f) Court-ordered support for other children which is actually paid.

(g) Spousal support paid pursuant to a court order from a previous marriage or the marriage before the court.[150]

Consult with your attorney to find out what is considered when determining gross and net income for child support in your jurisdiction. There may be other factors your court considers.

In Florida, each parent's net income is added together to get a combined net income. The parents or their attorneys then refer to a chart that lists the predetermined support amount based on that combined income and the number of children. Florida has a child support guidelines chart that provides the support schedule for parents whose combined net income ranges from $800 monthly to $10,000 monthly, with one to six children. The amount of income over $10,000 follows a formula that gets fed into the rest of the guideline calculations. For example, for one child, the multiplier would be 5%, and for two children, it would be 7.5%. Child support is then determined by using each parent's pro rata percentage of income to the total combined net income. Many other jurisdictions also have charts, but their numbers will differ from Florida. Your lawyer can provide you with the formula for your jurisdiction.

In Florida, the court is allowed to deviate plus or minus 5% from the guidelines without making factual findings giving a special reason why child support is not the exact guidelines amount. For cases where the difference exceeds 5%, the judge must provide written findings explaining why applying the guidelines amount is unjust or inappropriate. Other jurisdictions may have similar flexibility.

OVERNIGHTS CAN MATTER IN SUPPORT CALCULATIONS

Florida statutes have a special method incorporated into the calculation called the "gross-up" method that can help ensure fairness in child support. In the broadest strokes, under the gross-up method, when parents have roughly equal incomes and roughly equal amount of time-sharing, then child support becomes close to $0, because neither parent is fiscally better off, and thus better able to pay, or they are spending much more time with the children and thus spending much more money to provide for the child during that time. Similarly, the gross-up method also accounts for those cases where one parent earns significantly more and/or one parent really does have more than 50% time-sharing. A parent with greater income and fewer overnights is going to be paying significantly more, both for being the higher earner and to compensate for having little time with the children. Even where the higher earner also has most of the time-sharing, the gross-up method calculations can still lead to a support payment being made to the parent with much less time because of the consideration that the lesser-earning parent still needs some fiscal help.

Since the gross-up method uses a series of calculations that compare income and overnights of time-sharing, it was understood from the outset that truly enormous differences in income can distort the intent of the method, as well as one parent having very little time-sharing, which for this purpose is 20% of overnights in Florida. When the number of overnights gets too low, the formula flat out breaks, because the child support award grows unfairly large, so the 20% minimum is used for this method to prevent that breakage. Check with your lawyer to learn if a similar method is used in your jurisdiction.

CHILDREN WHO BENEFIT FROM "GOOD FORTUNE"

What happens to children of a multimillionaire parent whose income is well in excess of any of the children's reasonable needs? "The child is only entitled to share in the good fortune of his parent consistent with an appropriate lifestyle."[151] This means the child would, for example, be able to attend private school or participate in expensive extracurricular activities.

When the marriage of Diane and James dissolved, their three children benefited from their father's good fortune, as James's net monthly income was $453,483. This would have obligated James to pay $44,680 monthly if applying a strict mathematical application of the child support guidelines. However, James and Diane had an agreement requiring him to pay $12,000 monthly, and James also paid indirectly at least $16,770 monthly for medical and dental insurance costs; private school for all the children; and college tuition, fees, books, and room and board for the oldest son. When Diane sought to increase child support, the general magistrate found the children's needs were met, and so her request for an increase was denied and the denial was affirmed on appeal.[152]

Where there is support in excess of the children's needs, part of the excess may be ordered to be put in trust for the children, with a court-appointed guardian for the children's property.[153]

INSURANCE CONSIDERATIONS FOR ALIMONY AND CHILD SUPPORT

A trial court can require the paying spouse to carry life insurance securing alimony, child support, or both. This may occur when the paying spouse has a dangerous job, is old, or is in ill health. In Florida, the judge must make a finding as to the amount of such life insurance needed, the cost of insurance, and the insurability of the party ordered to obtain it.[154] The court may apportion the costs of insurance to either or both parties based upon each party's ability to pay.[155]

In closing, remember, you must specifically request the judge for any and all types of support that are appropriate in your case since the judge is not a mind reader and many jurisdictions do not allow a judge to award unrequested relief. Those who do not ask do not get, and so long as what you intend to ask for can seem reasonable, then ask away.

COSTLY MISTAKES MADE IN MARITAL SETTLEMENT AGREEMENTS

THE FIRST RULE OF MARITAL SETTLEMENT AGREEMENTS: *NEVER* SIGN AN agreement prepared by your spouse's attorney without having your own attorney review it and discuss it with you. Your spouse's attorney is looking out for their client's best interests—not yours!

Most settlement agreements will cover issues of support and equitable distribution of the parties' assets and liabilities. Assets that may be included are cash on hand or in bank accounts, stocks and bonds, retirement plans, business interests, vehicles, boats, planes, furniture and home furnishings, electronics, collectibles, jewelry, and real estate, as well as contingent assets. It may also address the parties' debts, including mortgages on real estate, auto loans, credit card debt, other judgments, contingent liabilities, and any other obligation pertinent to the parties' situation. The agreement can require that neither party incur any indebtedness for which the other party could be liable, except what is already expressed in the agreement.

The parties may elect to agree to health, life, or other types of insurance, who may be required to pay taxes and get tax refunds, and attorney's fees and costs. They may agree to waive any and all rights to share in their spouse's estate, or claim of a right to elect or any interest in a will or codicil of the other party. The agreement will usually have a provision for mutual releases between the parties. It can also have a provision that if the parties reconcile, it in no way eliminates or affects any of the agreement's provisions.

There may be clauses addressing separation and noninterference or mutual restraining orders, including agreements to refrain from making derogatory or negative comments about the other party on social media, in audio or print publications, or anywhere on the internet. These clauses may also require the offending spouse to remove any such posts within thirty days of signing the agreement. These provisions could be enforceable by contempt and an award of attorney's fees against the party violating those terms.

The agreement should state that its provisions cannot be modified except by the fully informed written consent by both parties or by court order. The agreement should also include what jurisdiction's laws will govern the interpretation of the agreement and the venue if there are future disputes arising from the agreement's provisions—where future litigation will be held.

Provisions regarding the children may be included in the agreement or in a separate parenting plan, which was discussed in Chapter 12. However, those provisions, depending on the jurisdiction, will need to demonstrate to the judge as being in the children's best interests.

Decide who is considered to be the "drafter" of the agreement. If only one side is deemed the drafter, then the language in all terms is construed against the drafter. For risk-mitigation purposes in most cases, it is better for the agreement to state that neither side is considered the agreement's drafter, regardless of who is writing the majority of the terms.

Throughout the years of practicing law, we have seen many agreements that, instead of resolving issues, cause additional post-dissolution litigation. The following are examples of what to do to avoid costly mistakes.

AVOID COOKIE-CUTTER AGREEMENTS

You want to include clauses in your agreement that specifically apply to your own situation. For an example of a religious aspect to be covered by agreement, a Jewish woman going through a divorce may want to insist that her husband agree to her obtaining a Get, a Jewish divorce document that effectuates a religious divorce between the parties. Without it, a rabbi might refuse to officiate a religious ceremony should the former spouse want to remarry. Since the husband must give the Get, which the wife receives and accepts, if it is not agreed to in writing before the parties' divorce, a now ex-husband who wants to cause his ex-wife pain may later make it difficult or impossible for her to get the Get.

If you have agreed that alimony payments are either modifiable or non-modifiable, that should be included in the marital settlement agreement. This clause can have significant consequences; it could be favorable to the party paying alimony if the receiving former spouse can never seek to increase the non-modifiable alimony award, or unfavorable if financial circumstances change so that the paying party later finds it difficult to keep paying.

If the alimony provision in the martial settlement agreement is modifiable, it usually addresses termination in the event the spouse receiving alimony remarries or the spouse paying alimony dies. You may want to consider adding a clause terminating alimony if the receiving spouse engages in a supportive relationship for a certain amount of time, or if the relationship meets certain other criteria. Florida has a specific statute that mandates the court to reduce or terminate an award of alimony upon a finding that a supportive relationship exists based on eleven factors, and this or something similar can be used to inform your position for an agreement.[156]

You may also want to consider how retirement will affect alimony, especially if the paying spouse is nearing retirement age. In many jurisdictions, this can otherwise be a means to modifying alimony.

In Florida, by statute, alimony can be reduced or terminated upon a judge finding the paying former spouse has reached retirement age by considering ten factors.[157] Lastly, you can also address the issue of the receiving spouse going back to work or making additional money after the agreement is signed. You can decide if those additional funds will or won't be a basis for modification.

An issue may be whether a spouse who changed names wants to keep the married name or revert back to their maiden name. Keeping the married last name avoids the hassle of changing all identification like a driver's license, other legal documents, credit cards, accounts, and anything name based. Then again, the easiest time to change a name back is as part of a divorce, rather than later going through a whole new court proceeding to change it afterward. Even though in many jurisdictions, the other spouse has no input during a divorce regarding whether the married name is kept or changed back, when there is a settlement agreement, it tends to incorporate this as a provision, rather than the spouse who took on the married name asking for it to be considered separately by the judge during the divorce.

Make Sure All Assets Referred to in the Agreement, Like Insurance Policies, Still Exist

Our firm was involved in a case where elderly parties agreed in a mediation for the marital settlement agreement to provide for life insurance "in existence," as there had been such a policy for many years. However, the policy was canceled by the husband shortly *before* the mediation, and as a result, the wife got no life insurance to secure the alimony obligation. A slightly different generalized wording in the agreement, such as, "the husband shall continue to maintain all life insurance policies that the parties have traditionally maintained in the amount of 'X' dollars and shall provide yearly proof of payment and a copy of the declaration page of the life insurance policy showing its renewal within 'Y' number days of the payment," would likely have preserved the need for the husband to get a replacement policy. Better still would be confirming the specific policy as part of the negotiation.

So often, parents don't think about the eventual and high cost of auto insurance when their children have not yet reached driving age. However, this can add many thousands of dollars yearly, even if the children never have an auto accident. How will this insurance be paid for? Who will be purchasing cars for the children, and is there an agreement on the type of car to be purchased as well as whether it will be a new or used vehicle?

Other insurance policies should be considered as well. One rarely thought-of example applies to "key man" insurance when distributing a family business. This insurance can cover the equalization payment related to distributing that business to protect the receiving spouse in case the payor dies before the debt is fully paid.

As pointed out in Chapter 16 on housing, you should meet with your insurance agent to determine, based on the age of your home and other factors considered by the insurance companies in your jurisdiction, whether you will need a new roof or other repairs or replacements in order to maintain insurance. So often, one party may end up with the house as part of their equitable distribution, only to find out that they have not budgeted the funds to pay for the substantial added expenses of a new roof or other major home repair. If this is recognized prior to entering into an agreement, the expected cost of this expense can be negotiated.

Another issue that we have often seen that is not addressed when one party is living in the home is who pays for the home expenses until it is sold. The agreement should spell out who pays the mortgage, taxes, insurance, and other carrying costs. Consider who is responsible to pay for repairs and what dollar amount requires mutual agreement before making a repair. The same applies to investment properties that are being sold.

Read the Entire Agreement Word for Word and Always Ask Questions If You're Not Sure About the Legalese

You want to have a comfort level before signing the document. Don't be afraid to question the lawyer if something doesn't seem right or might appear to be left out. Compare all the terms against a checklist of all the matters you want covered and/or were able to negotiate to conclusion. Make sure it is all in the agreement, as there have been cases where a lawyer accidently omits items in the agreement that were agreed to or that a party felt entitled to have.

Make Sure There Is Matching Mutual Intent on Terms or Provisions in the Agreement

Additional and unnecessary litigation can occur when the parties later disagree as to the intent or meaning of a particular part of their agreement. For example, the marital settlement agreement should clearly state valuation dates and specific dollar amounts for each asset and debt included in the distribution. Beyond bank accounts, stock portfolios, retirement accounts, and other similar items, apply the same consideration to any valuable property that is potentially subject to meaningful changes in value over time. The reason for this is simple: the values for some assets may be worth significantly more or less on the date of distribution or the date when the agreement is signed compared to the filing date of the petition for marital dissolution. You want to avoid additional litigation and expense in fighting over what dates were intended in valuing each of the items that would end up in dispute. You also need to decide if you will be splitting each asset or liability 50/50, by some other percentage, or by a specific dollar amount for the valuation date.

Spell Everything Out—Don't Think That the Parties Will Later Consider a Missing Item or Term as Part of the Agreement

Janice and Christopher entered into a marital settlement agreement where the split between the parties for a tax liability was omitted, and because of the type of asset, the liability fell solely on Christopher. Christopher later claimed he and Janice had agreed to each pay half of the liability, while Janice's position was that she never intended to share in that or it would have been included in the agreement. The judge reviewing the agreement determined it to be unambiguous and found in Janice's favor.[158]

Don't Forget to Address QDROs (If Pertinent to Your Case)

Qualified Domestic Relations Orders (QDROs) are the method by which retirement accounts are divided in a divorce. However, prior to entering the final divorce judgment, the parties should check with the company's Plan Administrator for the spouse whose retirement plan is to be divided, to make sure the QDRO gives effect to the parties' equitable distribution scheme. We have often seen the parties have the court enter a QDRO prematurely, only to later find out that the order's structure was unworkable for the participant spouse's company. This can result in additional time and expense to have a QDRO's defects remedied. When including a QDRO in a marital settlement agreement, you should be sure to include the amount to be transferred (which can be a mathematical formula rather than a specific dollar amount) to the nonparticipant spouse, which party bears the responsibility for obtaining the QDRO, and who pays the costs for obtaining it.

It is essential to put the Plan Administrator on notice that the parties plan on dividing the retirement asset in a QDRO by providing them a copy of the draft of the QDRO. Especially if a final divorce judgment is entered prior to the QDRO being completed and approved by the Plan Administrator, the participant spouse could elect to retire, which could eliminate the nonparticipating spouse being able to obtain survivor benefits. If the participant spouse dies, the entire account could be transferred to the participant's estate. The participant spouse could also take out a loan against the retirement plan, or withdraw all of its funds, to deprive the nonparticipant spouse.

Generally, many divorce attorneys utilize the services of an attorney or other professional specializing in handling QDROs.

Don't Sign an Agreement Before Having It Reviewed by a Lawyer and If Your Attorney Advises You Not to Sign, Trust Their Judgment—That's Why You Hired Them

We've seen costly mistakes when spouses sign agreements without consulting a lawyer, or when they disregard their lawyer's advice and sign a bad or unfavorable agreement anyway.

Don't let yourself be talked into signing a bad agreement by your spouse, or a family member, or because you're tired since you've been dealing with it for more than twelve hours straight that day. One mistake we have seen is when a spouse signed an agreement without first speaking to a lawyer. The spouse was "informed" about only so much being available for distribution or that "x" amount of alimony will be paid while the payor keeps most or all of the assets. The spouse might also have been convinced about not being entitled to some property like a pension or 401(k). Once the agreement is signed and the Final Judgment is entered, it is normally too late to fix, even on appeal, regardless of how badly that spouse was shortchanged.

Another unfortunate mistake is when the client signs an unfavorable agreement against the advice of their attorney. When Amy handled divorces in the trial court, she advised a client not to sign a marital property settlement agreement, but the client did so anyway against Amy's strong objection. Amy wrote a detailed letter to her regarding what could go wrong if the client signed the agreement, and Amy had her client countersign the letter. About six months later, the client called to tell Amy that everything she warned her about came to pass and how sorry she was that she didn't listen to Amy's advice. When Amy hung up she was relieved about writing the detailed letter which the client had acknowledged at that time, knowing that if there was no letter, her phone call would have taken a very different tone. The client would have accused Amy of not warning her about the negatives in signing the agreement, and Amy might have even been sued for malpractice.

Some attorneys concerned about their clients accepting an unfavorable agreement have even hired videographers to film the attorney going over each and every page of the document with the client before the client signs and asking to confirm with each term if this is what the client wants. The bottom line is to think very carefully before signing an agreement against the express advice of your attorney, as you may live to regret it!

Reread the Agreement at the End of the Negotiation Before Signing It, Including Attachments Like Equitable Distribution Schedules, and Never Sign Unless All the Referenced Exhibits Are Attached in Full!

All too often, costly mistakes occur by not rereading the marital settlement agreement one more time before signing it.

Through the years many unhappy, potential clients seeking appeals complain they signed a marital settlement agreement without the exhibits being attached to the document at that time, and when they later received the complete agreement, to their horror, they discovered items on the lists were not what had previously been discussed. We have had cases where a client who signed an agreement later believed the opposing counsel changed some of the terms, values, or dates just before providing the final draft to be signed. Arthur and Melanie discussed and agreed he would be paying her $5,000 monthly for 84 months. It was late at night after an exhausting mediation, and neither Arthur nor his attorney re-read the agreement. However, several days later, upon reading the agreement, he discovered that the agreement called for him to pay alimony of $6,000 a month for 84 months. Melanie maintained that $6,000 per month was what the parties agreed, leading to costly litigation.

IN SUMMARY

These have been just a sampling of the unfortunate situations we have seen which could have been avoided by: carefully thinking through all the terms to be considered, having your lawyer craft the terms to avoid unnecessary risks, and always rereading the agreement with all the attachments before signing it.

CHAPTER 23

PRENUPTIAL AGREEMENTS AND POSTNUPTIAL AGREEMENTS

THE NAME OF THE AGREEMENT TELLS YOU EXACTLY WHAT IT MEANS. "Nuptial" means marriage while "pre" means before and "post" means after. So, a prenuptial agreement (sometimes called an antenuptial agreement as "ante" also means before) are contracts about marriage entered into before getting married, while a postnuptial agreement is one entered into after getting married, and for the purposes of this chapter, before filing for divorce. Postnuptial agreements can have a great deal of overlap with settlement agreements, but for purposes of this chapter are agreements that were entered into while parties still had the intention to remain as a married couple.

At least in Florida, it is a requirement that prenuptial agreements and postnuptial agreements must be in writing. Even if your jurisdiction allows for oral nuptial-related agreements, you do not want to trust a he-said she-said situation years, if not decades, after the fact as to who exactly said and agreed to what provisions; it's better to keep the final version as a written, signed document.

In Florida, nearly any term that is not against public policy can be included in a prenuptial agreement, meaning about the only things that cannot be included are terms related to committing a crime; waivers of temporary support during a divorce (including temporary attorney's fees); most matters that would affect minor children's interests (such as child support or timesharing); and for Florida agreements entered into after October 1, 2007, when a state statute changed, leaving the other spouse so poor following divorce that he or she will be forced onto public assistance. Practically anything else is fair game. This tends to include the following:

EQUITABLE DISTRIBUTION

This is possibly the item most usually thought of when it comes to these agreements. Rather than each side pooling their property and/or treating any assets acquired during the marriage as marital, these agreements can easily have language to the effect of "what's mine is mine and what's yours is yours." The spouses in these agreements might want absolutely everything to remain separate, with no assets ever being considered marital, possibly except for later explicitly agreed to items. Just in case, such agreements should also probably specify that any increase or enhancement in value remains separate or some courts could treat the value increase as marital. Other agreements make carveouts for certain specific property such as a house, a business, or an inherited item that might otherwise too easily end up being thought of by somebody as marital. Everything that applies to assets also applies to debts; delineating which debts are shared, which debts are separate, and which debts, even if separate, would be partially or wholly guaranteed by the other spouse.

Yet more agreements have specific schedules as to who gets what upon divorce. These agreements can even have asset tables and timetables where for every year, or two, or ten of marriage some certain amount of money or other assets will be distributed to a spouse. This may potentially seem like alimony, but is just as different as dogs are from cats, which as with other pets are also property that can be handled in a nuptial agreement, so long as your jurisdiction allows it.

Distribution can include payments to third parties. As indicated above, paying off a debt—whether credits cards, car loans, mortgages, medical bills or nearly any other obligation—can fall under this category. Other payments would include money for other family members whether that be setting aside money to care for an aging relative or making payments to cover the ever-escalating cost of college and graduate school tuition for an adult child.

There can be additional, conditional triggers and clauses that tie different amounts or types of distribution to something non-monetary, like marital fidelity or something blatantly fiscal, like the performance of a portfolio investment, a business, or career advancement.

ALIMONY

Waiving alimony is an item that is frequently negotiated for in these agreements. Keep in mind though that one major limitation in Florida—along with any other jurisdiction that adopted the Uniform Premarital Agreement Act—is that following the adoption of that Act if a waiver of alimony in a prenuptial agreement makes one spouse eligible for some form of public assistance, then notwithstanding the agreement's terms the court can award alimony to the extent necessary to avoid having that spouse be eligible for public assistance. While that limitation acts as a sort of floor on how poor somebody can be left post-dissolution without alimony, at least in Florida there is another major type of alimony that cannot be waived. Spouses have a special duty to support each other during the marriage, and until the dissolution judgment is final a trial court can award reasonable temporary alimony. Your jurisdiction, if not in Florida, might have a related limitation on waiving alimony during the marriage.

A similarly common provision, as waiving alimony, is defining in advance how much alimony will be awarded. This amount can be as generic as a flat dollar figure per month or rely on some formula such as no alimony if married for less than five years, and then $1,000 per month plus another $1,000 monthly for every two full years of marriage thereafter. The duration of alimony can also be predetermined for either a fixed length of time, or following whatever formula to which the parties agree. All of the same types of alimony discussed in the alimony chapter are, in Florida, fair targets for negotiation. Just as with distribution, there can be other special factors that influence the type, amount, and duration of alimony, with a lapse in fidelity being a clear contention. Kandice had a provision in her agreement providing for a cost-of-living increase, but (showing how word choice matters) that increase did not start accruing with the signing of the agreement and only triggered with the final judgment of divorce, about a dozen years later.[159]

Alimony can be made non-modifiable as if set in stone, generally modifiable, modifiable only in certain, specific conditions, or non-modifiable under certain conditions. An example of the last item was in a case where an agreement had been reached that even if the wife returned to work as a nurse, that would not constitute grounds to modify alimony, although changes in employment are normally one of the most basic reasons to modify alimony in Florida.[160]

INHERITANCES

This involves agreeing in advance how property will be divided in the event of the other party's death. Sometimes that means agreeing to a specific set of property to be passed on, or a trust established, or life insurance to be put in place with a spouse named as the beneficiary. On the other hand, in Florida, it can include waiving the spouse's guaranteed minimum share of a deceased's property called the elective share. These effects can continue during a marriage or be timed to only trigger in the event of divorce. A person might think this is redundant compared to a will. However, wills are easy to change right down to the very moment a spouse leaves the room; after the "old" will was executed and witnessed, a new, replacement materially different will with very different terms might be put in place. Contracts, like nuptial agreements, are going to require joint participation by both spouses to change.

ATTORNEY'S FEES

Post-dissolution fees are a routine component in these agreements. Fee provisions tend to come in two types: either each side pays their own fees or the agreement contains a prevailing party provision. Prevailing party provisions come in multiple varieties and care should be taken to select the most appropriate type. For example, fees for prevailing when enforcing the agreement sounds the same as fees for prevailing when the agreement is breached, but there can be many hearings where there was no breach of the agreement (like a hearing to resolve conflicting values for an asset) and thus no fees. There can be fees for prevailing to defend the agreement, but again, in Florida, that is not as broad as enforcement. Broader still would be a prevailing party provision related to any litigation between the parties to the agreement concerning the agreement.

This section started with post-dissolution fees because in Florida, attorney's fees at issue in the middle of a dissolution action are not waivable, nor are prevailing party provisions for those fees enforceable. Your jurisdiction might be different, but in Florida those fees are considered part of the duty to support a spouse while still married by providing reasonably equal access to the courts. After the marital dissolution, that duty ends, and fees provisions become acceptable.

MINOR CHILDREN'S INTERESTS

For any jurisdiction that has signed the Uniform Premarital Agreement Act, no prenuptial agreement can adversely affect the right of a child to support. That removes very nearly all possibility of waiving child support. Even agreements that provide more child support than required by the guidelines might be adversely affecting the rights of a child who rather than needing the overage agreed to happens, due to a special circumstance, to need much more than even that. In Florida, this also applies to postnuptial agreements. Unless your attorney has a strong reason to give you the go-ahead, refrain from shortchanging your children.

DIVORCE SOS

The same logic holds for time-sharing and parenting plans. Private agreements between spouses are not automatically in the children's best interests. These require court approval. All the same rules and circumstances discussed in the chapter on time-sharing apply here. The closest an agreement can come for time-sharing, parenting plans, and child support is to have prospective language that would only become effective subject to the court finding such terms are in the children's best interests. Even then, those terms tend to act more as a starting point for the judge's decision-making rather than being guaranteed for inclusion in the final judgment.

CHOICE OF LAW AND SEVERABILITY

These terms determine which jurisdiction's law to apply regardless of where the legal dispute involving the agreement happens to be occurring and allow the rest of the agreement to survive even if one or more parts of it are discarded by the trial court.

The topics listed above are some of the more common items found in nuptial agreements. The parties are free to include whatever other terms about which they can agree so long as the jurisdiction of the contract allows for it.

These agreements, once entered into, are treated like other contracts, and a court in Florida will not rewrite them so the terms of the agreement take precedence over how a judge might otherwise rule. When one judge tried to award a wife lump sum alimony for money she lost during the marriage, that judgment was reversed on appeal because this was an impermissible attempt by the trial court to modify a prenuptial agreement with an alimony waiver provision.[161] Also, like other contracts, the law requires a need for consideration—something of value exchanged between the parties to a contract. For a prenuptial agreement, that consideration is normally the act of getting married. While the parties might well be in love, in lust, or both prior to getting married, from a legal perspective neither side owes the other any special duty. Because, as an unmarried couple, no special duty is yet owed, negotiating a prenuptial agreement is considered to be an arm's length transaction as with most other contracts. Conversely, an already married couple is treated as also being in a fiduciary relationship with each other for postnuptial agreements because, despite how the parties to a marriage may sometimes view the other spouse, the relationship is deemed to be nonadversarial, with mutual trust and confidence.[162] Moreover, while consideration might be refraining from filing for divorce, it can also be an agreement to get something of value, like trading one property right for another.[163, 164]

The question arises as to why anybody would even consider entering into a postnuptial agreement. The big reason for a prenuptial agreement is obvious—at least one of the two spouses-to-be is refusing to get married without having this agreement—but for postnuptial agreements the parties are already married. One common reason a postnuptial agreement might come about is because one spouse got caught cheating, and the price to remain married (besides a renewed commitment to faithfulness) is signing an agreement that will bring financial pain in a later divorce should that spouse be found to be cheating again. As another example, after roughly twenty years of Deborah and Alvin's marriage, that was then deteriorating, Deborah proposed a postnuptial agreement in which Alvin agreed to give her additional equity in the marital home based on how the first mortgage would be paid off, and he waived all interest in her pension plan.[165] Irrespective of Deborah filing for divorce about a month later, the appellate court ordered the trial court to find the agreement as binding on the husband.

Maybe one spouse is about to engage in a risky investment or start a new business and the other spouse wants specified financial protection or an escape vehicle should the investment start to go poorly. Having an agreement that transfers assets or an income stream out of the marriage to the noninvesting spouse can be a security measure or asset-protection vehicle. This can also prearrange matters in case of divorce, in recognition of just how stressful investments and business ventures sometime can become. The flip side of that coin is a prospective business partner might insist on there being an effective agreement before letting the spouse join or invest to keep the business out of any later divorce.

As the reader of this book, you are more likely to be considering how to get out of or maintain an agreement than just learning about them for the first time. Challenges to an agreement can be made by alleging there was duress, coercion, overreaching, fraud, or unconscionability/ unfairness.

Duress

Duress is an imposed condition where a person cannot freely act of their own volition to reject a contract. The classic example is the threat not to get married unless the other party signs the prenuptial agreement. However, the circumstances of the demand must be considered because the threat in isolation is not enough. For example, fifteen minutes before walking down the aisle is likely to be considered duress, while fifteen months before the wedding and before a venue has even been selected likely will not be treated as such. When Jerald handed over a prenuptial agreement at 11:30 p.m. the night before Susan was going to marry him at their Las Vegas wedding, that was duress.[166]

Coercion

Coercion is similar to duress but not quite as forceful. When Magda challenged her prenuptial agreement, the trial court correctly found she was not under duress, but the appellate court reversed with a finding that she was coerced.[167] Magda was a religious woman, and she was still dealing with the trauma that came with being persuaded by Paul to have an abortion following their premarital relations, yet two weeks later, he preyed upon her turmoil and used the additional context of an upcoming emigration hearing to induce her to sign a prenuptial agreement.

Overreaching

Overreaching means being able to force the other person into an unfavorable agreement; this tends to overlap with coercion and duress. It can also be applied when somebody is placed into a clearly impossible position. Suzanne proposed an agreement drafted by an attorney, while Terry was unrepresented, that obligated him to deed over the house, take on all the family's debts, give her the better vehicle (while he kept a car worth $500), pay a significant portion of her attorney's fees, and pay more in support than he earned in a regular work week.[168] All of this was found to be an overreaching agreement.

Additionally, the combination of duress, coercion, and overreaching tend to be pled as a trio. This is so that if the facts of the case fail to fit one legal term, they might apply to another of the three.

Fraud

Fraud normally comes in the form of misrepresenting the terms or effect of the agreement or otherwise being deceptive about the circumstances to trick the other person into signing it. Hiding substantial assets or income can also potentially count as fraud, since the other party might have insisted on very different terms if that party knew the real financial picture. Being a few dollars off on a checking account that varies from month to month is probably immaterial, but purposefully refraining from disclosing assets showing you are worth several times what is listed or overstating some debt to make your financial picture look worse than it really is all to induce somebody into taking less alimony or a smaller amount of equitable distribution are strong indicators of fraud. One case that seemed to ride the line was when Michael left his pension plan off his financial disclosure to a prenuptial agreement while listing his 401(k) and other assets.[169] Both the trial and appellate courts found his wife, Mary Lou, had enough of a general and approximate knowledge of Michael's financial resources for this lapse not to count as fraud or misrepresentation based on the rest of the disclosure and the comparative smallness of the pension. The dissenting appellate judge disagreed because the pension was still a six-figure asset.

Postnuptial agreements have all the same requirements as prenuptial agreements, but with one important extra addition: the parties are no longer at arm's length, and each side owes the other a fiduciary duty of disclosure. There is no hiding that you've just won the lottery, that you've gotten stock in a company about to go public, that your business is much more valuable than your spouse might think, or that some relative has just left you a large inheritance.

Unconscionability

An agreement can also be challenged if it is unconscionably unfair such that no reasonable person would normally agree to it. Florida courts look to when the prenup was entered into, rather than the financial position of the parties at the time of the divorce, when deciding whether the agreement is fair. This charge primarily acts as a means to switch the burden of proof. Should the circumstances show the agreement is truly unfair, it becomes the responsibility of the person benefitting from the unfair agreement to show there was full and fair disclosure or disclosure was only waived in writing because the challenging spouse already had had adequate knowledge of the property and obligations at issue. Because nondisclosure easily feeds into a fraud-based challenge, it is generally far better to be honest and up-front when disclosing one's finances than to rely on a waiver, especially when the agreement is going to be unfair to the person to whom disclosure is not being provided.

Honesty is the best policy, especially with disclosure. Parties have a great deal of freedom to draft a wide variety of prenuptial and postnuptial agreements, given the specifics of your jurisdiction. Bear in mind that the best way to preserve an agreement is to have full disclosure and reasonable ability to review and negotiate, with at least some fairness in the agreement. The best way to strike or void a portion, if not the whole of the agreement, is to show the opposite—that disclosure was lacking.

PART 3

MISTAKES TO AVOID
WITH APPEALS

CHAPTER 24

WHAT ARE APPEALS AND WHY DO THEY MATTER?

IN THE FILM *WAITING TO EXHALE*, A WIFE NAMED BERNADINE, PLAYED BY Angela Bassett, is told by her husband that he is leaving her for another woman. The following day, while her husband is at work, Bernadine, in a fit of rage, goes into her husband's large walk-in closet, rips his suits off their hangers, and empties from his closet all of his clothes and shoes, which she throws into his BMW through the sunroof. She then lights the car on fire and smokes a cigarette while watching it all burn.

This dramatic scene, although cathartic for the character, would have real-life consequences in the context of a divorce. Her husband could claim her behavior is so erratic that she needs to have a psychological evaluation. He could seek temporary custody of their children based on this display of violence and also seek to have her barred from the marital home. At the final hearing, he could seek an unequal share of the marital assets, claiming she intentionally dissipated marital assets by setting his car on fire and causing his personal property to literally go up in smoke.

What could Bernadine do if a judge entered orders granting each of her husband's requests? *She could appeal*!

This chapter will educate you on the various types of Florida appeals that can be used during the divorce litigation and after the final judgment is entered. These are not in-depth explanations, as we could write an entire book on this topic. As explained in the Introduction, we are appellate attorneys with vast experience in this area of the law. About half of our practice is devoted to family law appeals, as well as advising and assisting divorce lawyers during their clients' divorce litigation.

WHAT IS AN APPEAL?

An appeal is a proceeding undertaken by a party who seeks review from a higher court to reverse or set aside/vacate the decision of a lower court. The party who is taking the appeal is called the Appellant or Petitioner, and the opposing party is called the Appellee or Respondent. If the Appellee or Respondent is also unhappy with part of the order or judgment, a cross-appeal can be undertaken.

There are multiple types of appeals, which have different rules that apply to them, depending upon whether the appeal is a final appeal, a nonfinal (interlocutory) appeal or a writ. However, unlike trial court proceedings, in civil appeals, like appeals in family law cases, there is no discovery, nor are there multiple hearings. Depending on the type of appeal—such as an appeal from a final judgment—the case is decided primarily on the appellate record and just one set of documents called "briefs," which are not always brief in size!

An appeal matters because it gives the Appellant a second chance, if successful. Otherwise, the trial court's decision will stand and likely have significant impact on the litigant's life.

In the United States, most jurisdictions adhere to precedent, which means the judges decide appeals by following the opinions in published cases, which are themselves other, earlier appellate decisions. From the many thousands of cases that are published, an experienced appellate attorney will know how to find, and be able to find, those cases having similar facts to the client's issue on appeal and that were decided favorably.

Appellate courts have rules and procedures that must be followed when practicing before them, which tend to greatly differ from trial courts. Because of the nature of the appellate process, most family law attorneys will recommend that a client seek an experienced appellate lawyer when there is the possibility of an appeal. For some divorces that are expected to be extremely hard-fought from the outset, an appellate attorney may be brought in early to the divorce proceeding for their legal expertise and to provide the necessary support that will lead to a more favorable, or at least less unfavorable, appellate record in case there is an appeal.

The names of the appellate courts differ from state to state. For example, in Florida family law appeals, the litigant will appeal from the Circuit Court, which is the trial court, to the District Court, the intermediate appellate court. The highest appellate court in the state is the Supreme Court of Florida. In New York, the trial court is called the Supreme Court.

APPEALS AND PETITIONS FOR WRITS BEFORE FINAL JUDGMENT IS ENTERED

Most people think that an appeal is only filed after a final judgment is entered. There are also certain types of appeals that may be filed during the divorce. While not every order that is entered is appealable, knowing which orders are and the type of appeal that can be filed is the province of a skilled appellate attorney.

Writ of Certiorari

In Florida, Angela Bassett's character Bernadine could seek review of the order requiring her to undergo a psychological evaluation for setting the car on fire by filing a petition for writ of certiorari. In order to prevail using this form of review, the Petitioner must show the trial court's order departs from the essential requirements of law and results in material injury that cannot be remedied on an appeal after the final judgment is entered. However, because this writ is discretionary, even when the petition meets those requirements, an appellate court may still deny the requested relief. In Florida, the petition must be filed within thirty days of the rendition of the order being appealed.[170]

Certiorari review is most often utilized to challenge discovery orders, such as requiring a party to turn over sensitive documents, medical records, their lawyer's work product, and/or information protected by attorney-client privilege. The attorney will make what is referred to in legal circles as the "cat out of the bag" argument. Once the information is disclosed to the other party, it can't be undisclosed from them, and taking an appeal after the final judgment is entered cannot ever fix that.

Certiorari can be used for certain other issues. Wallace and Brittany had a son. When this child was about four years old, Wallace sought to establish a time-sharing/visitation plan, resulting in Brittany absconding with the child to Pennsylvania. It took Wallace four long years to find his son, and he was able to retrieve him after filing an emergency pick-up order that was granted. However, less than two weeks later, while the child was back in Florida with his father, Wallace read on social media that Brittany was en route to take back the child! Wallace then filed an emergency ex-parte verified motion for temporary injunction and other orders, seeking to temporarily prevent Brittany from again removing the child from Florida and to prohibit contact between her and the child due to a perceived imminent danger to the child.[171] Although Wallace had been expecting a one-hour hearing, it was set on the trial court's five-minute motion calendar. Rather than deciding Wallace's injunction motion at the hearing, the judge expressed frustration that no time-sharing order had been entered and, without either party requesting it, ordered the child returned to Brittany, allowing her to take the child back to Pennsylvania.

That same day following the hearing, Wallace filed an emergency petition for writ of certiorari, claiming the judge violated his right of due process. The very next day, when Wallace had been directed to return the child to Brittany by 5:00 p.m., the appellate court temporarily stayed the trial court's order, pending the higher court's ultimate determination. The appellate court requested to see the hearing's transcript (and fortunately, a court reporter was present at that hearing). The appellate court agreed with Wallace and quashed the trial court's order that would have required him to hand the child over to Brittany.[172]

Writ of Mandamus

In the context of divorce, mandamus is used to enforce a legal right by compelling a judge to perform a duty required by law. One of the most basic requirements of mandamus is for the judge's action to be ministerial, since the judge cannot have any discretion in the matter. Seeking the relief of a writ of mandamus is improper if any other adequate remedy can get results. It also cannot be used to enforce rights between private parties—mandamus lies only against a public official or a governmental agency. Although mandamus is most commonly used to force the issuance of a license or a permit, it has also been used in divorces to force the judge to hold the hearing so that a final judgment may be entered.

Allan, who wanted to divorce his wife, had a problem. He had requested the trial court hold a final hearing in his dissolution of marriage, but he was an inmate in Florida's correctional system. Allan filed a motion to schedule a final telephonic hearing, but the trial court denied the motion, finding that sworn testimony was necessary to accomplish this, and also declining to order Allan be transported to attend the final hearing in person. Allan sought relief through a writ of mandamus. The appellate court agreed with Allan, granted the writ, and ordered the trial court to schedule a final hearing with Allan appearing by telephone.[173] The judge had no discretion to keep Allan from the divorce to which he was entitled.

Writ of Prohibition

Writs of prohibition most commonly occur in divorce cases to disqualify a judge. This remedy will not be successful if you want to disqualify the judge just because of one or even several adverse rulings. If that were the case, the appellate courts would be flooded with appeals attempting to have judges disqualified, and would result in forum shopping for a different judge they believed would be more favorable to their position. To be legally sufficient, a motion for disqualification must assert a well-founded fear in the mind of a party that he or she will not receive a fair and impartial trial before that judge. The fear cannot be merely subjective; the motion must allege facts, which if accepted as true, would prompt a reasonably prudent person to fear they could not get a fair trial.[174]

An allegation that a trial judge is a "friend" on Facebook with an attorney appearing before that judge, standing alone, is not a sufficiently legal basis for disqualifying that judge.[175] However, the content of communications through Facebook might be a basis for disqualification. Prior to entering a final judgment in a divorce case, a judge reached out to the wife, ex parte, in the form of a friend request. On the advice of her attorney, the wife did not to respond to this invitation because she would be engaging in ex parte communications with that judge. Ex parte communication can be considered highly prejudicial by the other party and so is usually avoided. Thereafter, the trial court's final judgment attributed most of the marital debt to the wife and provided her husband with a disproportionately excessive alimony award. When the trial court denied her motion to disqualify, she filed a petition for writ of prohibition. The appellate court agreed with the wife, finding that she was put in the untenable situation of either engaging in ex parte communications with the judge or not responding to the invitation, which created a reasonable fear of offending the soliciting judge.[176]

Another example of a successful disqualification concerns Bruce and Emily. Bruce's initial filing for an injunction against Emily was successful, and he was awarded 100% time-sharing/custody of the couple's children. Emily thereafter filed for a divorce, but over the ensuing four years, was unable to have Bruce be personally served with the divorce paperwork. Emily requested a status conference before the judge to whom both the divorce and injunction cases had been assigned. At that hearing, the judge's frustration with the lack of service was evident, as the judge made a number of unsolicited comments that Bruce was trying very hard to evade service. The judge called Bruce's actions ridiculous and outrageous and then said if Bruce was an uncooperative witness in a criminal case, the judge could have him arrested, and the judge would research whether he had this power.

It didn't end there. The judge stated Bruce must be a wealthy husband, even though there was no financial evidence in the record, and that Bruce took control over the situation by getting the domestic violence injunction. The judge further opined Bruce was abusing the system and wondered if dissolving the injunction would allow the court to make all those findings disappear. Finally, the judge issued an order to have a hearing in the injunction case on all matters related to time-sharing/custody and support, despite there being no pending motions for the court to rule on and Emily not having made such request. It is apparent from these facts that there was a legally sufficient basis for the appellate court to find Bruce had a well-founded fear of not getting a fair and impartial trial. The petition was granted, and the case was remanded back to be heard by a new judge.[177]

Habeas Corpus

"The writ of habeas corpus is a high prerogative writ of ancient origin designed to obtain immediate relief from unlawful imprisonment without sufficient legal reasons. Essentially, it is a writ of inquiry and is issued to test the reasons or grounds of restraint and detention."[178] In our practice, we have sought this writ when a client is improperly jailed for contempt. One such improper basis is being jailed for failing to make an equitable distribution cash payment.

Petitions for the various writs are filed directly in the appellate court and include the facts of the case and the entire argument within the petition itself. Except for a petition for writ of certiorari, at least in Florida, there is no jurisdictional deadline for filing. However, you don't want to delay filing for any of the writs, as the perception may be that the longer you wait, the less important the requested relief really is. Along with the petition, you must prepare and file an appendix, which includes the various trial court filings that becomes the appellate record used by the court to decide the writ.

Interlocutory Appeals

Remember Bernadine, the wife who burned all her husband's clothes in his convertible? If he obtained a temporary parenting plan giving him all the overnight time-sharing/visitation with the children and limiting her to supervised daytime time-sharing/visitation, she could appeal that nonfinal order. She could also appeal an order awarding her husband temporary sole and exclusive possession of their marital home to live in with the children.

While each jurisdiction will have its own limits on appealable non-final orders, Florida's rules of appellate procedure detail an exclusive list of the orders that can be reviewed by interlocutory appeal.[179] They include orders that concern venue; grant, continue, modify, deny, or dissolve injunctions, or refuse to modify or dissolve injunctions; that determine the right to immediate possession of property; that grant or deny a motion to disqualify counsel; that determine jurisdiction over the person; and a number of other types of orders. In family law matters, the appellate rules allow appeals from nonfinal orders that concern:

- the right to immediate monetary relief;
- the rights or obligations of a party regarding child custody or time-sharing under a parenting plan; or
- that a marital agreement is invalid in its entirety.

The process and procedure for taking this appeal is different than those of the various writs. Since it is jurisdictional (controls the ability of a court to actually consider the matter), a Notice of Appeal for a nonfinal order must be filed within thirty days of the rendition of that order. Otherwise, you will be unable to appeal the order until the very end of the case, unless it is modified by the judge during the litigation. In Florida, a Notice of Appeal is simply a notice informing the trial and appellate courts of the order being appealed, the date the order was rendered by the lower tribunal, and the nature of the order. Unlike petitions for writs, in Florida, you file your Notice of Appeal in the court where your case is proceeding (for divorce, it is the Circuit Court), and the clerk of that court transfers the Notice of Appeal to the relevant district court that will decide the appeal.

Instead of including your entire argument in that notice, you file separate legal briefs, which include the facts of the case, the issues to be decided, your legal argument, and the conclusion, which requests the decision or action you want from the appellate court. Appellate courts generally have established rules as to the maximum size of briefs in either page count or word count. There is also likely to be a specific timeframe under your jurisdiction's rules for the filing of each brief. In Florida, the parties must also prepare an appendix from court filings, which serves as the appellate record for the appellate court to review in deciding the case. Moreover, certain jurisdictions, like Florida's appellate courts, will not automatically stay the trial court's proceedings simply because an interlocutory appeal is ongoing in the appellate court. In such circumstances, the trial court can proceed with very nearly the whole case, even having the final hearing or trial, but cannot enter a final judgment. Depending on your jurisdiction, you would need to directly request the trial court stay some or all of the proceedings while the appeal is pending.

APPEALS FROM FINAL ORDERS

Television and movies often make it appear that the appeal is filed on day one, the next day the parties are arguing their case before a panel of appellate judges, and the judges orally announce their decision at the conclusion of the argument or by written opinion soon thereafter. But that is far from the reality of what actually occurs in an appeal. In Florida, an appeal from a final judgment can easily take 18 months to more than

2 years. However, an appellate court might expedite certain family law appeals upon request, like some appeals involving children's issues.[180]

At the final hearing in the divorce action, Bernadine's husband can seek unequal distribution by claiming a "dissipation of marital assets," the legal term in Bernadine's case for her destruction of her husband's property. Suppose the judge only awarded her husband $1,000 for all his destroyed clothes and the car in the final judgment. Her husband could appeal this judgment by timely filing a Notice of Appeal. However, before actually filing the notice, there is one extremely important document his lawyer should file first—a Motion for Rehearing.

MOTIONS FOR REHEARING

Divorce trials are normally fact intensive. The testimony of each spouse may be at odds with the other. The determinations of need and ability of the spouses as testified to by forensic accountants for each of the parties could be significantly different. Then there are the business appraisers, vocational experts, and real estate appraisers who may all have contrary views depending upon whom they are testifying for. The trial court judge must listen to the testimony and consider evidence presented by the parties and the other witnesses, observe their demeanor, and determine credibility.

The appellate court is a reviewing court, and, depending on the issue to be reviewed, is there to determine if the trial judge made erroneous rulings that require reversal, abused their discretion, or made rulings unsupported by competent substantial evidence. Appellate courts want the trial judge to have a final opportunity to correct mistakes made during the divorce proceedings. This is accomplished by having the party that is not satisfied with the rulings in the Final Judgment file a Motion for Rehearing.

Unless there is an error clearly shown on the face of the judgment (like a mathematical error), motions for rehearing should be filed before appealing. At a major family law conference in Florida, one of the speakers made it clear that an attorney would be committing legal malpractice by failing to file a motion for rehearing.

In some states, the time for filing a motion for rehearing comes shortly after a final judgment is entered. In Florida, a motion for rehearing must be served within 15 days from the date the final judgment is filed with the Clerk of Court. The judgment is usually filed the same day it is signed, but occasionally it may be filed later.

Motions for rehearing should include every possible issue you believe the trial judge got wrong or omitted from the final judgment, not just ones that your trial counsel thinks are the most important, or that can be won on a motion for rehearing. In fact, while most motions for rehearing are denied, they are still additionally useful to file because:

1. The judge may agree with some of your arguments, and you may get relief.

2. You can include every perceived erroneous ruling in a motion for rehearing, since depending on the issue, an appellate court may treat an issue not raised in rehearing as waived or unpreserved for appeal. That means the appellate court would flat-out refuse to consider the waived issue if you tried to raise it in your final appeal. There have been cases where the appellate courts refused to even consider agreed stipulations made by the parties that were orally recognized by the trial judge but inadvertently omitted from the final judgment.[181] A common reversible error is when a judge's oral pronouncements at trial are inconsistent with the written final judgment. However, if not included in a motion for rehearing, it could be considered waived.[182] In one case, the trial attorney did not raise the failure of the judge to award the wife alimony because the attorney thought a motion for rehearing would not prevail on this issue, but this caused collateral damage because appellate counsel were later precluded from raising alimony in the appeal.

3. Motions for rehearing provide an opportunity to build up your eventual appellate record. When contacted about taking an appeal by a potential client, we often get permission from the client to speak with the trial attorney so we can hash out various issues that might otherwise be overlooked in the motion for rehearing. Sometimes we are able to advise the client to file an affidavit or add other documents to the motion which then ultimately result in getting a reversal based on the enhanced record's contents.

Check with your attorney regarding the necessity of filing a motion for rehearing in your jurisdiction.

FILE YOUR APPEAL ON TIME!

Once the trial judge rules on the motion for rehearing, if the party is still unhappy with the decision, an appeal may be taken. It is crucial to speak with an appellate attorney to make sure the appeal is timely initiated. In Florida, filing an appeal from a final judgment is jurisdictional, meaning if your Notice of Appeal is filed late, your appeal will be dismissed and you will be unable to have your case reviewed by the appellate court. You are out of court forever for that appeal. In one case, the opposing party filed the Notice of Appeal through the court's electronic filing portal late at night, but it was not actually filed until 12:02 a.m. on the 31st day. Although just two minutes late, the appellate court determined it lacked jurisdiction and dismissed the appeal. The takeaway is for you to check with appellate counsel to determine the time for filing an appeal from the order you are unhappy with. You never want to have to face the fact that you have lost the right to appeal because it was untimely filed.

If you are the one filing an appeal, your now former spouse can cross-appeal if also unhappy with parts of the judgment. They would have had to file their own motion for rehearing or face the same appellate consequences in not requesting rehearing.

You can seek to stay the final judgment while the case is on appeal by first requesting it in the trial court. In Florida, should the judge deny the motion to stay the judgment, you can separately ask the appellate court to review that denial within the existing appeal. The trial court may decide to stay part or all of the order or judgment with the requirement that a bond be posted or other relevant conditions be imposed to obtain the stay. You need to check the rules in your jurisdiction to determine what conditions will apply.

THE APPELLATE RECORD

Our law firm has worked with divorce attorneys throughout trial court proceedings to ensure that the client has the strongest record possible in case there is an appeal by either party. Many judges request that trial counsel representing the parties each submit a proposed Final Judgment for the court to have when deciding the case. Trial counsel may need to be reminded to include in the proposed judgment that the judge "reviewed the whole court file," as this will allow appellate counsel to more freely use all documents filed with the court during the divorce proceedings. As appellate counsel, we have found many gems when having the ability to utilize information from the entire court file.

In Florida, the appellate record consists of the proceedings at the trial court level, which generally include a copy of the trial court docket and portions of the court file of that case, such as the petition, answer, motions, orders, hearing transcripts, and exhibits. Unlike the other types of appeals, the record in final judgments from divorce cases is prepared by an appellate clerk who works in the circuit court. The Florida Rules of Appellate Procedure sets forth the type of documents that are automatically made part of the appellate record by the circuit court clerk.

You can file "Directions to Clerk" to request additional court documents—such as depositions, interrogatories, or other discovery materials filed during the divorce proceeding—be included in the appellate record. At least in Florida, those types of filings are not made part of the appellate record unless specifically requested. Where necessary, you can also curtail the record by delineating which filings you want to exclude from it. Because the opposing party also has the opportunity to add additional filings as well to the record, when you desire to exclude filings, it is usually better to individually list every last document to be included in the record rather than requesting a standard record minus some items. The appellate courts, when considering the filed briefs, won't normally review any trial court documents or evidence outside of the appellate record. If critical documents were never filed or presented to the trial judge in a family law case, they can almost never be made part of the appellate record.

THE BRIEFS

Unlike the trial court, which is before one judge, in the Florida District Courts the appeal will be decided by a panel of three judges. In the trial court, there is the petition or complaint, answer, counter-petition, motions, discovery, lots of communication between attorneys, and multiple court hearings with witnesses testifying and evidence presented. Rather than a multitude of filings over the course of litigation, the appeal is mainly decided on the appellate record and the briefs.

Briefs generally follow the same format and requirements as interlocutory appeals, except for the timeframe for filing the Initial Brief. Only the Initial Brief is actually required. The Answer Brief and Reply Brief are optional, but it is highly recommended that they be filed; otherwise, the appellate court will only have the Appellant's initial version of the facts and law. The Initial and Answer Briefs are required to include standards of review, which affect the way the appellate judges perceive the facts and legal arguments. Many inexperienced lawyers do not apply the correct standard of review, which can make the lawyer's own case unnecessarily difficult and/or make the appeal easier for the other side.

ORAL ARGUMENT

In Florida, the hearing called "oral argument" is discretionary with the appellate court, and frequently there may be no oral argument at all during the entire appeal from a divorce related case. If oral argument is granted in a family law appeal, it is usually limited to just one session before the panel of three judges who will be deciding the case. At oral argument, there are no witnesses and no testimony is taken. Each party has a set amount of time during which his or her attorney will be asked questions by the judicial panel regarding the case. The judges may want clarification of a legal point or fact that was brought up during the lower court proceedings, or they may ask questions about other published opinions from cases that may have been referred to or discussed in the briefs. In Florida, most District Court oral arguments are scheduled from 10 to 20 minutes per side. The appellate attorneys should know the record cold and be prepared for the judges to ask most anything about the case, including what precise page in the record a fact can be found or on which an argument is premised. Since the time provided for oral argument is short, the attorneys are expected to be able to immediately answer any question.

ATTORNEY'S FEES AND COSTS

Attorney's fees are normally awarded by statute or by contract. Florida has a specific statute that permits awards of attorney's fees at both the trial and appellate courts in family law cases. In an appeal, the request for appellate attorney's fees must be timely filed by a separate motion and not included in the brief, otherwise it won't be considered. In Florida, the motion for appellate attorney's fees is one area where a litigant can include material that is germane to the motion but was not previously before the trial court.

Usually, the appellate court rules on the request for attorney's fees around the same time it issues the decision on the merits of the appeal. In Florida, inexperienced lawyers will often seek costs incurred as part of the appeal in their motion for appellate attorney's fees. Specifically, "taxable costs" including filing fees, fees for preparation of the appellate record, any hearing or trial transcripts necessary to determine the proceedings, bond premiums, and other costs permitted by law are sought by filing a separate motion in the trial court. More general costs—such as in-office photocopies and printing—when able to be pursued, are also sought at the trial court level, along with the motion to enforce the order that granted appellate attorney's fees. This can cause a disconnect because the appellate order addresses only "fees," while in the trial court you would be seeking "fees and costs."

THE APPELLATE COURT DECISION

This is the waiting game. We have received the appellate court decisions in as little as two days after an oral argument or as long as a year and three months after the Reply Brief was filed. The decision may totally affirm the trial court's order or judgment; may partially affirm and partially reverse the judgment; or may totally reverse, quash, or vacate the judgment. In Florida, sometimes the appellate court will issue a written opinion, and at other times will only affirm the trial court's order without any further explanation, except possibly just a case citation.

MOTION FOR REHEARING

In Florida, if you believe the appellate court, in rendering the opinion in your appeal, has overlooked or misapprehended something then you can file a motion for rehearing to address that issue. Unless your jurisdiction allows for it, the motion for rehearing should not look like it is merely rearguing the same points you already argued in the appeal.

Another type of rehearing is a request for your case to reheard *en banc*, which means to have all the judges in your appellate court review the case. In Florida, *en banc* consideration is only given by the whole appellate court when the matter is considered to be of great public importance or when the opinion in your case is contrary to another opinion previously issued by that appellate court.

There may also be other types of post-appellate motions that can be filed, depending upon the procedural rules of your jurisdiction.

THE MANDATE

This is the official document that concludes the appeal and ends the appellate court's jurisdiction over the appeal. The mandate vests jurisdiction back to the trial court to proceed with the case in accordance with the decision/opinion of the appellate court.

IN SUMMARY

This chapter has merely touched on some of the appeals that can be taken. Each one has specific rules and procedures that apply. It is most important for you and your lawyer to work with an appellate attorney so mistakes can be avoided, as an appeal is normally the last chance to fix something that has gone wrong in your case and these mistakes can make otherwise appealable issues absolutely unfixable.

In one divorce case, the client came to us after a judge had found him in contempt and wanted to appeal the order. Unfortunately, his trial attorney thought the order was final, when it was actually an interlocutory order. The divorce attorney had filed what was titled as a motion for rehearing, expecting to extend the time for filing the appeal of a final judgment. However, as there are no rehearings from interlocutory orders in Florida, the motion did not toll the time, and the potential client found out he was unable to appeal the contempt order. He was devastated as a result of the burdens the contempt order had placed on him.

Because the appellate process is very complicated, a knowledgeable and experienced appellate attorney is essential, and most family law attorneys will recommend their client seek the help of an appellate attorney when there is the possibility of an appeal.

THE NEXT STEPS NOW THAT YOU'VE BEEN THROUGH THIS JOURNEY

FIRST, WE WANT TO THANK YOU FOR READING THIS BOOK. YOU SHOULD now be better prepared to develop a plan that will lead you to a successful divorce, while keeping your sanity throughout this process. If you have children, we hope you will now have a better understanding of how to guide them through this process and help them feel more secure so the trauma of a divorce will be less.

However, we certainly cannot promise that going through a divorce will be painless. Think about what is important to you. Unless you are prepared to spend an exorbitant sum on legal fees, be prepared to compromise on some of the issues, especially the ones you really don't care about as much. In addition to spending thousands of dollars on issues big and small, there is a price to pay on your physical and emotional health. Save your battles for those issues that are truly meaningful to you. You need to face the fact that you probably won't get everything you want.

After the final judgment of divorce is entered, your divorce journey may still not be at an end if there is an appeal. Be sure to follow the suggestions in Chapter 4 and adapt them for hiring an appellate lawyer that specializes in divorce so you can optimize your chances of appellate success.

Finally, as one lawyer who has been through the divorce process not once but twice, and as another lawyer who is a child of divorce, we can tell you that although no one escapes divorce totally unscathed, the future can be bright.

You are now able to write your own story. Give yourself a happy ending. You deserve it.

As stated in the Introduction, we are appellate lawyers and do not directly represent clients as trial court divorce lawyers. Please do not contact us for the purpose of handling your divorce in the trial court. Should you want to get in touch with us regarding an appeal or to have us work with your divorce attorney so they can access our expertise, have your attorney consult with us. Please visit the book's website at *www.divorcesosbook.com*; our website at *www.shield-levine.com*; or LinkedIn at *www.linkedin.com/in/amy-shield-6606a111/*.

ACKNOWLEDGEMENTS

Thank you to L.A. Perkins, who was always willing to listen and provide valuable information about her publishing journey, and who introduced us to Ashley Mansour, our writing coach who made this book possible. Many kudos to Jessica Reino, our editor supreme, who had boundless enthusiasm and astute comments that improved the content and overall structure of our book. And thank you to Victoria Woodruff for so aptly managing the publishing process, promptly answering all our questions, and keeping us on track.

We want to especially thank our wonderful early readers, Lee Burke, Hope Firsel, Kurt Heide, Alyssa Reiter, and Hadas Stagman, for their time in reading our manuscript and for the many suggestions we incorporated in the book. Each was chosen for their particular expertise in their respective professions, and the constructive feedback we received was invaluable. We additionally want to thank Linda Buccilli, Laurie Dubow, and Leorah Greenman for their friendship and generosity. Finally, thank you to Anh Thu Le for her insightful opinions, which greatly helped in finalizing the book's photographs and title.

ABOUT THE AUTHORS

AMY SHIELD, ESQ., IS AN EXPERIENCED FLORIDA ATTORNEY SINCE 1976, whose practice encompasses all facets of family law appeals including alimony, child support, custody (time-sharing), division of property (equitable distribution), prenuptial and postnuptial agreements, relocation, supportive relationships, and contempt orders. She has also been appointed as guardian ad litem and attorney ad litem by the court in contested time-sharing cases. Amy has handled hundreds of appeals throughout Florida, and first argued before Florida's highest court, the Supreme Court of Florida, at 28 years old. She has received an AV Preeminent® rating—the highest rating from Martindale-Hubbell for legal expertise, communication skills, and ethical standards, which is awarded to approximately 10 percent of all United States attorneys. She was also recognized as a top appellate lawyer in 2025 by *Palm Beach Illustrated*.

ABOUT THE AUTHORS

Roger Levine, Esq., a Florida appellate attorney, also has an AV Preeminent® rating from Martindale-Hubbell for achieving the highest level of professional excellence in legal knowledge, communications skills, and ethical standards. Besides representing clients throughout Florida in appeals involving all facets of family law, divorce lawyers rely on his expertise as their "lawyer's lawyer," and he advises them about the law on legal issues that arise in their practice, drafts memorandums of law they will give to the judges, and when requested, attends hearings with trial counsel to advise on the spot about intricate areas of law and make sure all important points are covered at the hearing. Roger has also given back to the community, having served as a guardian ad litem to dependent children in Palm Beach County for approximately ten years. Roger has similarly been recognized as a top appellate lawyer for 2025 by *Palm Beach Illustrated*.

ENDNOTES

1   For more than 135 years, Martindale-Hubbell has been evaluating attorneys for their strong legal ability and high ethical standards through a Peer Review Rating system. Prior to the 1887 edition of Martindale's American Law Directory, which was the first publication to provide such ratings to attorneys, there was no way of truly knowing if the lawyer you were considering doing business with was trustworthy, ethical, or skilled in the legal field. *See* https://www.martindale.com/ratings-and-reviews.

2   Guardian ad Litems and Attorney ad Litems are discussed in Chapter 13.

3   *In re Estate of Magee*, 988 So. 2d 1 (Fla. 2d DCA 2007); §732.201, Fla. Stat. (2024) and §732.2065, Fla. Stat. (2024).

4   *J.N.S. v. A.M.A.*, 194 So. 3d 559, 562 (Fla. 5th DCA 2016).

5   *Buschor v. Buschor*, 252 So. 3d 833 (Fla. 5th DCA 2018).

6   *See* the TalkingParents website for more information about this app at https://talkingparents.com and https://ourfamilywizard.com for more information about co-parenting on the OurFamilyWizard website.

7   Black's Law Dictionary 399 (12th ed. 2024).

8   https://www.myflfamilies.com/services/abuse/domestic-violence.

9   §934.06, Fla. Stat. (2024) states in part that whenever any wire or oral communication has been intercepted, no part of the contents of that communication and no evidence derived from that communication may be received in evidence in any trial, hearing, or other proceeding in or before any court.

10 §934.03, Fla. Stat. (2024) provides that the offense for illegally intercepted wire, oral, or electronic communications can be a misdemeanor of the first degree or a felony of the third degree, depending on the circumstances involved.

11 §934.10, Fla. Stat. (2024).

12 *O'Brien v. O'Brien*, 899 So. 2d 1133 (Fla. 5th DCA 2005).

13 §775.083, Fla. Stat. (2024) and §934.03, Fla. Stat. (2024).

14 Christopher B. Hopkins, *Discovery of Facebook Contents in Florida Cases*, 31 No. 2 Trial Advoc. Q. 14 (2012).

15 *Nucci v. Target Corporation*, 162 So. 3d 146, 153-54 (Fla. 4th DCA 2015). The *Nucci* opinion cites to cases in New York, New Jersey, Michigan, and California.

16 Fla. R. Civ. P. 1.280(b)(1).

17 Black's Law Dictionary 1695 (12th ed. 2024).

18 Black's Law Dictionary 1695 (12th ed. 2024).

19 *See* Endnote 1.

20 §44.405, Fla. Stat. (2024).

21 *Amalgamated Transit Union, Local 1579 v. City of Gainesville*, 264 So. 3d 375, 380 (Fla. 1st DCA 2019); *Perera v. Genovese*, 345 So. 3d 882, 891 (Fla. 4th DCA 2022).

22 Serenity Gibbons, *You And Your Business Have 7 Seconds To Make A First Impression: Here's How To Succeed*, Forbes (Jun. 18, 2018), https://www.forbes.com/sites/serenitygibbons/2018/06/19/you-have-7-seconds-to-make-a-first-impression-heres-how-to-succeed/

23 An attorney can instruct a deponent not to answer only when necessary to preserve a privilege, like an attorney-client or work product privilege, to enforce a limitation on evidence directed by the court, or to suspend the deposition if the examination is being conducted in bad faith or in an unreasonably annoying, embarrassing, or oppressive manner. Fla. R. Civ. P. 1.310(c) and (d). Henry P, Trawick, Jr., *Florida's Practice and Procedure*, §18:8 Oral Depositions (2025 ed.). In Florida, it is improper for attorneys to generally instruct their witness not to answer a question during that witness's deposition. *Smith v. Gardy*, 569 So. 2d 504, 507 (Fla. 4th DCA 1990).

24 Fla. R. Civ. P. 1.310(e) governs witness review of their deposition.

25 There are exceptions, such as where the error is apparent on the face of the judgment, like a clear mathematical error made by the judge in calculating alimony or child support. In Florida, your attorney could file a "Statement of the Evidence" for the appellate court, but this is a very poor substitute for a transcript of the proceedings.

26 §61.13 (3)(a-t), Florida Statutes (2024).

27 *Akre-Deschamps v. Smith*, 267 So. 3d 492 (Fla. 2d DCA 2019).

28 More on therapy in Chapter 13.

29 Social investigations and guardians ad litem are discussed in Chapter 13.

30 In some jurisdictions, children are not considered adults until they turn twenty-one years old. You should check with your attorney to find out at what age a child is no longer considered a minor.

31 A parenting plan may state: "When the parents are using an alternating weekend plan and the holiday schedule would result in one parent having the child for three weekends in a row, the parents will exchange the following weekend, so that each has two weekends in a row before the regular alternating weekend pattern resumes."

32 CPIAP's website within state.gov informs the program "allows the Office of Children's Issues to contact the enrolling parent or legal guardians when a passport application is submitted. They do this to check if the two-parent consent rule for children's passports have been met." Only U.S. citizens under the age of 18 can be enrolled. For questions about the program, call 1-888-407-4747 or email PreventAbduction1@state.gov.

33 *Tucker v. Liebknecht*, 86 So. 3d 1240 (Fla. 5th DCA 2012), holds the appropriate measurement for distance is a straight-line rather than one based on roads and driving distances. The *Tucker* case cites to cases in Connecticut, New York, and Ohio.

34 §90.503, Fla. Stat. defines a psychotherapist as a person authorized to practice medicine in any state or nation; a person licensed or certified as a psychologist; and a person licensed as a clinical social worker; each of whom is engaged in the diagnosis or treatment of a mental or emotional condition, including alcoholism and other drug addiction.

35 §90.503(2) & (3), Fla. Stat. (2024).

36 *"ad litem"* is a Latin term that literally means "for the suit." Black's Law Dictionary 53 (12th ed. 2024).

37 Victoria Sexton, *Wait, Who Am I Representing? The Need for States to Separate the Role of Child's Attorney and Guardian Ad Litem*, 31 GEOJLE

831 at FN 4 (Fall, 2018).

38 §61.401, Fla. Stat. (2024).

39 In Florida, by statute the guardian ad litem "when appointed shall act as next friend of the child, investigator or evaluator, not as attorney or advocate but shall act in the child's best interests." Section 61.403, Fla. Stat. (2024).

40 Section 61.403, Fla. Stat. (2024).

41 Traditionally, hearsay is testimony or a written document that is provided by a witness who relates not what he or she knows personally but what others have said, and that is therefore dependent on the credibility of someone other than the witness. Such testimony or information is generally inadmissible under the rules of evidence. *Hearsay*, Black's Law Dictionary 864 (12th ed. 2024). If inadmissible, hearsay cannot be considered by the trial judge.

42 Florida Family Law Rule of Procedure 12.364, and Section 61.20(1), Fla. Stat. (2024).

43 §61.20(1), Fla. Stat. (2024).

44 §61.20(2), Fla. Stat. (2024).

45 Fla. Fam. L. R. P. 12.285(d) & (e).

46 Forensic accountants analyze financial data and provide expert testimony in legal cases.

47 *Finch v. Cribbs*, 376 So. 3d 63 (Fla. 1st DCA 2021).

48 Black's Law Dictionary 937 (12th ed. 2024).

49 §61.30(2)(a)1-14, Fla. Stat. (2024).

50 The sample financial affidavit is an excerpt from the free Florida Family Law Financial Affidavit (Long Form) *See* Fla. Fam. L. R. P. 12.902(c).

51 Dorothy, from the film *The Wizard of Oz* (1939)

52 *See* Chapter 21 for more on alimony.

53 *Wolfe v. Wolfe*, 953 So. 2d 632 (Fla. 4th DCA 2007).

54 It can seem like there are always hurdles in trying to prove your income, and trusts have several. The loan originator may also want to see a 24-month history of the trust's income. Should your trust payments come

from the slow whittling down of an asset or investment in the trust, the originator may want to see these payments will keep being made for at least another three years, after accounting for any use of the trust to cover closing costs or a down payment.

55 Dissipation of marital assets is discussed in Chapter 19. Where this may become an issue later, the judge sometimes orders that the net proceeds from the sale of the house be held in escrow until this issue is resolved.

56 *Lift v. Lift*, 1 So. 3d 259, 260-61 (Fla. 4th DCA 2009).

57 *Manolakos v. Manolakos*, 871 So. 2d 258, 260 (Fla. 4th DCA 2004).

58 *Krakower v. Krakower*, 913 So. 2d 1212 (Fla. 4th DCA 2005).

59 *Guimbellot v. Guimbellot*, 352 So. 3d 950 (Fla. 1st DCA 2022). There was a reversal for only considering assets and not also liabilities in asset-based valuation approach.

60 *Held v. Held*, 912 So. 3d 637 (Fla. 4th DCA 2005).

61 *Adams v. Adams*, 340 So. 3d 551 (Fla. 2d DCA 2022).

62 *Adams v. Adams*, 340 So. 3d 551 (Fla. 2d DCA 2022).

63 *Kvinta v. Kvinta*, 277 So. 3d 1070, 1075-76 (Fla. 5th DCA 2019).

64 *Vanzant v. Vanzant*, 82 So. 3d 991, 992-93 (Fla. 1st DCA 2011). The judge reversed for having a judgment that appeared to simply split the difference between the husband's and the wife's valuation of their liquor store business.

65 Pets are so important to their owners that we have devoted a separate chapter to this topic.

66 Carolyn Osorio, *How Much Do Americans Spend on Their Pets?*, Money Digest, Feb. 29, 2024, 10:30 EST, https://www.moneydigest.com/1527893/how-much-money-do-americans-spend-pets/

67 One Pennsylvania appellate court noted that the former husband "is seeking an arrangement analogous, in law, to a visitation schedule for a table or a lamp," overlooking that any terms set forth in an agreement attempting to award custodial visitation with or shared custody of personal property are void. *Desanctis v. Pritchard*, 803 A. 2d 230, 232 (PA Super 2002).

68 *Bennett v. Bennett*, 655 So. 2d 109, 110 (Fla. 1st DCA 1995).

69 *Bennett v. Bennett*, 655 So. 2d 109, 110-11 (Fla. 1st DCA 1995); *Travis v. Murray*, 42 Misc. 3d 447, 459, 977 N.Y.S.2d 621, 631 (NY Cnty. Sup. Ct. 2013).

70 *Springer v. Springer*, 322 So. 3d 172 (Fla. 2d DCA 2021). In case you are wondering, the appellate court declined to hold Lizabeth in contempt.

71 Should you plan to argue the need for your pet as an emotional support animal, be aware that shortly after the trial in this case concluded, a Florida statute went into effect that criminalized a person's fraudulent proof or need for an emotional support animal. You need to check in your jurisdiction if there is a statute that also criminalizes falsely claiming to need an emotional support animal.

72 *Baggett v. Baggett*, 422 S.W.3d 537, 549-50, (Tenn. Ct. App. 2013).

73 *Hament v. Baker*, 97 A.3d 461 (Vt. 2014).

74 *Aho v. Aho*, 2012 WL 5235982 (Mich. Ct. App. 2012).

75 *Raymond v. Lachmann*, 264 A.D.2d 340, 695 N.Y.S.2d 308 (1st Dept. 1999); *Travis v. Murray*, 42 Misc.3d 447, 977 N.Y.S.2d 621 (NY Cnty. Sup. Ct. 2013).

76 *Travis v. Murray*, 42 Misc.3d 447, 977 N.Y.S.2d 621 (NY Cnty. Sup. Ct. 2013).

77 Domestic Relations Law § 236(B)(5)(d)(15). "in awarding the possession of a companion animal, the court shall consider the best interest of such animal."

78 Chapter 750 ILSC 5/503(n); Alaska Stat. §25.24.160(a)(5).

79 In re Marriage of Phalen, 2023 Il. App. (3d) 220296-U; 2023 WL 6249100 (2023).

80 Cal. Fam. Code § 2605.

81 Cal. Fam. Code § 2605(c)(1).

82 Stevens Scott Stephens, Marital and nonmarital assets - Family pets, 23 Fla. Prac., Family Law §11:13 (Nov. 2023 Update) and C.B-*C. v. W. C.*, 77 Misc.3d 342 178 N.Y.S.3d 386 (Supreme Court Nassau County 2022).

83 *Ballard v. Ballard*, 158 So. 3d 641 (Fla. 1st DCA 2014).

84 *Naylor v. Naylor*, 127 So. 3d 1288 (Fla. 1st DCA 2013).

85   *Coe v. Rautenberg*, 358 So. 3d 24 (Fla. 4th DCA 2023).

86   *Ridings v. Ridings*, 198 So. 3d 1128 (Fla. 4th DCA 2016).

87   *Moore v. Moore*, 543 So. 2d 252 (Fla. 5th DCA 1989).

88   *Austin v. Austin*, 120 So. 3d 669 (Fla. 1st DCA 2013).

89   *Williams v. Williams*, 163 So. 3d 1258 (Fla. 1st DCA 2015).

90   *Vickery v. Vickery*, 8 So. 3d 443 (Fla. 5th DCA 2009).

91   *Firestone v. Firestone*, 263 So. 2d 223 (Fla. 1972).

92   Some jurisdictions have laws about pet visitation schemes in similar form to time-sharing and parenting plans for children, while other jurisdictions, of which Florida is one, treat pets as any other property. *Bennett v. Bennett*, 655 So. 2d 109 (Fla. 1st DCA 1995).

93   *Gulbrandsen v. Gulbrandsen*, 22 So. 3d 640 (Fla. 3d DCA 2009).

94   *Roth v. Roth*, 312 So. 3d 1021 (Fla. 2d DCA 2021).

95   *Fawcett v. Gainey*, 214 So. 3d 793 (Fla. 5th DCA 2017).

96   *Fawcett v. Gainey*, 214 So. 3d 793 (Fla. 5th DCA 2017).

97   *Yon v. Yon*, 286 So. 3d 322 (Fla. 1st DCA 2019).

98   *Collier v. Collier*, 343 So. 3d 183 (Fla. 1st DCA 2022).

99   *Lakin v. Lakin*, 901 So. 2d 186 (Fla. 4th DCA 2005).

100 *Lyons v. Lyons*, 687 So. 2d 837 (Fla. 2d DCA 1996).

101 *Mondello v. Torres*, 47 So. 3d 389 (Fla. 4th DCA 2010).

102 *Jensen v. Jensen*, 824 So. 2d 315 (Fla. 1st DCA 2002).

103 *Ruberg v. Ruberg*, 858 So. 2d 1147 (Fla. 2d DCA 2003).

104 *McGowan v. McGowan*, 344 So. 3d 607 (Fla. 1st DCA 2022).

105 *Naranjo v. Ochoa*, 366 So. 3d 11 (Fla. 4th DCA 2023).

106 *Mills v. Mills*, 845 So. 2d 230 (Fla. 3d DCA 2003).

107 *Rogers v. Rogers*, 351 So. 3d 1230 (Fla. 2d DCA 2022).

108 *Lasset v. Lasset*, 768 So. 2d 472 (Fla. 2d DCA 2000).

109 *Thomas-Nance v. Nance*, 189 So. 3d 1040 (Fla. 2d DCA 2016).

110 *Harby v. Harby*, 331 So. 3d 814 (Fla. 2d DCA 2021).

111 *Crowley v. Crowley*, 678 So. 2d 435 (Fla. 4th DCA 1996).

112 Like so many things that can happen in a divorce, there are exceptions and depleting one account to pay living expenses post-petition while

purposefully accumulating without spending your routine paychecks that would otherwise have been spent on bills is a good reason for the court to stick with the account's earlier balance.

113 *Reese v. Reese*, 363 So. 3d 1202 (Fla. 6th DCA 2023).

114 *Rabbath v. Farid*, 4 So. 3d 778 (Fla. 1st DCA 2009).

115 *Johnson v. Johnson*, 847 So. 2d 1157 (Fla. 5th DCA 2003).

116 *Deasy v. Deasy*, 386 So. 3d 946 (Fla. 4th DCA 2024).

117 *Niederkohr v. Kuselias*, 301 So. 3d 1112 (Fla. 5th DCA 2020).

118 *Huntley v. Huntley*, 578 So. 2d 890 (Fla. 1st DCA 1991).

119 *DeLorenzo v. DeLorenzo*, 736 So. 2d 805 (Fla. 2d DCA 1999); *Zambuto v. Zambuto*, 76 So. 3d 1044 (Fla. 2d DCA 2011).

120 *Dampier v. Dampier*, 298 So. 3d 695 (Fla. 1st DCA 2020).

121 *Hines v. Williams*, 384 So. 3d 237 (Fla. 4th DCA 2024).

122 *Bellegarde v. Bellegarde*, 392 So. 3d 152 (Fla. 4th DCA 2024).

123 *Griffin v. Griffin*, 392 So. 3d 230 (Fla. 1st DCA 2024).

124 *Pringle v. Pringle*, 388 So. 3d 885 (Fla. 3d DCA 2023).

125 *Rogers v. Rogers*, 12 So. 3d 288 (Fla. 2d DCA 2009).

126 *Aronoff v. Aronoff*, 355 So. 3d 952 (Fla. 4th DCA 2023).

127 *Michener v. Michener*, 403 So. 3d 1040 (Fla. 3d DCA 2025).

128 *Konz v. Konz*, 63 So. 3d 845 (Fla. 4th DCA 2011).

129 NFTs, aka "Non-Fungible Tokens," are ownership rights to unique digital pictures that are publicly recorded on various cryptocurrency block chains. Because the individual pictures are theoretically unique, even if everyone else on the internet can still download and use them, these pictures are non-fungible, as they cannot be exchanged for another "identical" NFT. Thus any NFT, like the saying about snowflakes, is going to be different from every other NFT. Moreover, these digital ownership rights tend to be collected in the same manner as trading cards and paintings.

130 *Nassirou v. Borba*, 236 So. 3d 1180 (Fla. 3d DCA 2018).

131 Only for those plans that allow it, which will almost certainly exclude IRA-based plans.

132 *Graham v. Graham*, 123 So. 3d 625 (Fla. 1st DCA 2013).

133 While still married, if filing separately the $3,000 is instead $1,500 per year.

134 Black's Law Dictionary 92 (12th ed. 2024).

135 §61.08(3), Fla. Stat. (2024).

136 §61.071, Fla. Stat. (2024).

137 *Byers v. Byers*, 910 So. 2d 336 (Fla. 4th DCA 2005).

138 *Zalkin v. Zalkin*, 392 So. 3d 159 (Fla. 4th DCA 2024).

139 §61.08(6), Fla. Stat. (2024).

140 §61.08(7)(c), Fla. Stat. (2024).

141 §61.08(7)(d), Fla. Stat. (2024).

142 *Frechter v. Frechter*, 548 So. 2d 712 (Fla. 3d DCA 1989).

143 *Byers v. Byers*, 910 So. 2d 336, 342 (Fla. 4th DCA 2005).

144 *Byers v. Byers*, 910 So. 2d 336, 342 (Fla. 4th DCA 2005).

145 *Adelberg v. Adelberg*, 142 So. 3d 895, 897 (Fla. 4th DCA 2014).

146 *Middleton v. Middleton*, 79 So. 3d 836, 837 (Fla. 5th DCA 2012).

147 *Moody v. Newton*, 264 So. 3d 292, 294-95 (Fla. 5th DCA 2019).

148 *Welch v. Welch*, 951 So. 2d 1017 (Fla. 5th DCA 2007).

149 *Deoca v. Deoca*, 837 So. 2d 1137, 1139 (Fla. 5th DCA 2003).

150 §61.30(3), Fla. Stat. (2023).

151 *Miller v. Schou*, 616 So. 2d 436, 439 (Fla. 1993).

152 *Ferraro v. Ferraro*, 971 So. 2d 826 (Fla. 3d DCA 2007).

153 *Finley v. Scott*, 707 So. 2d 1112 (Fla. 1998).

154 *Byers v. Byers*, 910 So. 2d 336, 346 (Fla. 4th DCA 2005).

155 §61.08(4), Fla. Stat. (2023).

156 §61.14(1) (b), Fla. Stat. (2023).

157 §61.14(c)(1), Fla. Stat. (2023).

158 Legally speaking, because the court found the marital settlement agreement to be unambiguous, Christopher was disallowed from presenting parol evidence to prove his claim about the true intent of the parties.

159 *Francavilla v. Francavilla*, 969 So. 2d 522 (Fla. 4th DCA 2007).

160 *Jaffee v. Jaffee*, 394 So. 2d 443 (Fla. 3d DCA 1981).

161 *MacKaravitz v. MacKaravitz*, 710 So. 2d 57 (Fla. 4th DCA 1998).

162   *Baker v. Baker*, 394 So. 2d 465 (Fla. 4th DCA 1981).

163   *McIntyre v. McIntyre*, 824 So. 2d 206, 207-08 (Fla. 2d DCA 2002).

164   Waivers of the elective share are special in Florida in that pursuant to Section 732.702(3), Fla. Stat. no consideration other than signing a pre-nuptial or postnuptial agreement is required.

165   *Chipman v. Chipman*, 975 So. 2d 603 (Fla. 4th DCA 2008).

166   *Flaherty v. Flaherty*, 128 So. 3d 920 (Fla. 2d DCA 2013).

167   *Bates v. Bates*, 345 So. 3d 328 (Fla. 3d DCA 2021).

168   *Tenneboe v. Tenneboe*, 558 So. 2d 470 (Fla. 4th DCA 1990).

169   *Gordon v. Gordon*, 25 So. 3d 615 (Fla. 4th DCA 2009).

170   An order is rendered when a signed, written order is filed with the clerk of the lower tribunal. Fla. R. App. P. 9.020(h).

171   *Ex parte* is the term for not providing notice to the opposing party for actions or communication with the court. However, sometimes the court will require that the opposing side receive notice. Wallace and Brittany attended the trial court hearing by Zoom.

172   *Hodge v. Babcock*, 340 So. 3d 521 (Fla. 3d DCA 2022).

173   *Johnson v. Johnson*, 783 So. 2d 326 (Fla. 1st DCA 2001).

174   In Florida, Rule 2.330 of the Rules of General Practice and Judicial Administration lists a number of other grounds that may be pled when seeking to disqualify a judge.

175   *Law Offices of Herssein and Herssein, P.A. v. United Services Automobile Association*, 271 So. 3d 889 (Fla. 2018).

176   *Chace v. Loisel*, 170 So. 3d 802 (Fla. 5th DCA 2014).

177   *Higgins v. Higgins*, 275 So. 3d 204 (Fla. 5th DCA 2019).

178   *Henry v. Santana*, 62 So. 3d 1122, 1125 (Fla. 2011).

179   Fla. R. App. P. 9.130.

180   Judge Hugh Glickstein, who was an advocate for children, was upset that an appeal involving visitation took more than two years since the entry of the final judgment. He explained that the children were not frozen in time during the appeal, and a child's time was not an adult's time, and cited to a section of an article that stated: "Unlike adults, who measure the passing

of time by clocks and calendars, children have their own built-in time sense based on the urgency of their instinctual and emotional needs. What seems like a short wait to an adult can be an intolerable separation to a young child to whom a week can seem like a year and a month forever..." *French v. French*, 452 So. 2d 647, 651 (Fla. 4th DCA 1984).

181 *Fine v. Fine*, 308 So. 3d 172 (Fla. 4th DCA 2020).

182 *Eaton v. Eaton*, 293 So. 3d 567 (Fla. 1st DCA 2020).

www.ingramcontent.com/pod-product-compliance
Lightning Source LLC
Chambersburg PA
CBHW070548130626
46556CB00001B/58